FOR THE LOVE OF
CHILDREN

Register This New Book

Benefits of Registering*

- ✓ FREE **replacements** of lost or damaged books
- ✓ FREE **audiobook** – *Pilgrim's Progress*, audiobook edition
- ✓ FREE information about new titles and other **freebies**

www.anekopress.com/new-book-registration

*See our website for requirements and limitations.

FOR THE LOVE OF CHILDREN

More than 100 Inspiring
Stories for and about Children

Dwight L. Moody

We love hearing from our readers. Please contact us at www.anekopress.com/questions-comments with any questions, comments, or suggestions.

For the Love of Children – Dwight L. Moody
The stories in this book, with the exception of the biography in the back, are in the public domain.
Originally published by Rhodes & McClure Publishing Company, 1900, Chicago
Cover Design: J. Martin
Cover Photography: Inara Prusakova/Shutterstock
eBook Icon: Icons Vector/Shutterstock

Printed in the United States of America
Aneko Press
www.anekopress.com
Aneko Press, Life Sentence Publishing, and our logos are trademarks of
Life Sentence Publishing, Inc.
203 E. Birch Street
P.O. Box 652
Abbotsford, WI 54405

RELIGION / Inspirational
Paperback ISBN: 978-1-62245-561-4
eBook ISBN: 978-1-62245-562-1
10 9 8 7 6 5 4 3 2 1
Available where books are sold

Contents

Contents v
Preface ix
The Lost Kiss 1
The Happy Home 3
The Little Greyhound in the Lion's Cage 3
A Voice from the Tomb 5
The Boy that went West 6
The Speaking Card 9
The Imprisoned Children 10
Found in the Sand 11
Blind Bartimaeus 13
Higher and Higher 14
Hold Up Your Light 15
The Horse that was Established 16
The Hand on Moody's Head 17
The Idiot Boy 18
Believe 19
The Bible 20
Willie 21
Two Boys and Two Fathers 22
Little Great Men 24
The Demoniac 24
A Good Mother 26
In Jail 27
The Repentant Son 28

The Prodigal's Return	29
Very Sad News	31
The Little Orphan's Prayer	32
The Child Angel	32
Rover	34
Faith	36
Son, Remember	37
Reaping the Whirlwind	38
The Praying Little Cripple	39
A Boy's Victory	40
The Young Converts	42
Lost on the Deep	44
Looking Down from Heaven	45
Sunday School Love	46
The Little Norwegian Boy	47
Hold the Fort	47
The Collier and His Children	49
Young Moody's Conversion	51
A Little Child Shall Lead Them	53
A Mother Dies that her Boy may Live	54
Peace	55
Work Among the Street Arabs	56
Mrs. Moody Teaching Her Child	57
Dr. Booth's Story	59
Moody Chasing His Shadow	60
A Sad Story	60
The Dog Fighter	63
The Prisoner Weeping for His Children	64
The Child and President Lincoln	68
Moody in the Far West	69
The Little Orphan	71
Moody's Mother and Her Prodigal Son	73
Jump into Father's Arms	75
A Child Legend	76

Sammy and His Mother ... 77
A Singular Story ... 79
Humility ... 81
The Child and the Infidel ... 82
Picking up the Bible ... 84
Johnny Cling Close to the Rock ... 85
The Saloon Keeper and his Children ... 86
Love in a Sunday School ... 89
The Loved One and the Lover ... 91
The Cross ... 92
For Charlie's Sake ... 93
The Orange Boy ... 96
Finding Your Picture ... 99
A Bad Boy ... 100
Saved in Weakness ... 101
Young Moody at School ... 102
Child Friendship How Durable ... 103
The Blind Child ... 106
A Little Boy Converts his Mother ... 107
Sympathy ... 109
A Boy's Story ... 111
The Dying Sunday School Teacher ... 113
Prayer Answered ... 115
The Smiling Child ... 116
The Stolen Boy ... 117
Little Jimmy ... 118
Willie ... 119
The Child & the Book ... 120
Breaking the Tumblers ... 120
The Recitation ... 121
How Little Moody Took the Whippings ... 122
Dr. Chalmers' Story ... 123
Over the Mountains ... 124
The Smiling Mother's Sad Farewell ... 125

Off for America	127
Parting Words	128
Moody and the Children	129
The Drunken Boy Reclaimed	130
The Fatal Slumber	131
Open the Door	133
Obedience Explained	133
The Little Bird's Freedom	134
Over the River	135
Willie Asks Pardon and Prays	136
Waiting for Jesus	137
A Child's Request for Prayer	138
Emma's New Muff	139
Pull for the Shore Sailor	140
Young Moody in Boston	141
Dinna Ye Hear Them Coming	142
The Mistake that was Corrected	143
Let the Lower Lights be Burning	144
The Little Boy	146
Emma's Kiss	147
The Little Winner	148
Cherries	149
The Story of Moody's Life	151
Similar Updated Classics	191

Preface

Dwight L. Moody's sermons and counsel abounded in illustrations involving the youngest members of society. With him, as with the Master, the little child is a type of the kingdom. Hence his numerous touching stories about children. In this volume, the aim of the compiler has been to present these remarkable incidents connected with child life. In every instance the child is in the foreground of the picture and the great evangelist, in his own language, tells the story. Carefully selected from Mr. Moody's ministry at home and abroad, it is hoped that these true and wonderful stories may prove of special and personal interest to readers of all ages. This book also contains an overview of Moody's life and ministry. In the interest of the Savior's cause, the volume is dedicated especially to the children of America.

J. B. McClure.
Chicago, IL.

The Lost Kiss

I remember, a few years ago, that my little girl used to be in the habit of getting up cross some mornings. You know how it is; when any member of the family does not get up in a sweet temper, it disturbs all the rest of the family. Well, one morning she got up cross, and spoke in a cross way, and finally I said to her, "Emma, if you speak in that way again, I shall have to punish you." Now, it was not because I didn't love her; it was because I did love her, and if I had to correct her it was for the good of the little child. Well, that went off all right. One morning she got up cross again. I said nothing, but when she was getting ready to go to school, she came up to me and said, "Papa, kiss me."

I said, "Emma, I cannot kiss you this morning."

She said, "Why, father?"

"Because you have been cross again this morning. I cannot kiss you."

She said, "Why, papa, you never refused to kiss me before."

"Well, you have been naughty this morning."

"Why don't you kiss me?" she said again.

"Because you have been naughty. You will have to go to school without your kiss."

She went into the other room where her mother was and said, "Mamma, papa don't love me. He won't kiss me. I wish you would go and get him to kiss me."

But her mother said, "You know, Emma, that your father loves you, but you have been naughty."

So, she couldn't be kissed, and she went down stairs crying as if her heart would break, and I loved her so well that the tears came into my eyes. I could not help crying, and when I heard her going down stairs I could not keep down my tears. I think I loved her then better than I ever did, and when I heard the door close I went to the window and saw her going down the street weeping. I didn't feel good all that day. I believe I felt a good deal worse than the child did, and I was anxious for her to come home. How long that day seemed to me! And when she came home at night and came to me and asked me to forgive her, and told me how sorry she felt, how gladly I took her up and kissed her, and how happy she went upstairs to her bed!

It is just so with God. He loves you, and when He chastises you, it is for your own good. If you will only come to Him and tell Him how sorry you are, how gladly He will receive you and how happy you will make Him, and, oh, how happy you will be yourself.

The Happy Home

A little girl who had attended one of our meetings went home and climbed upon her father's knees and said, "Papa, you have been drinking again." It troubled him. If his wife had spoken to him, he might have got mad and gone out into some shop or saloon and got more liquor, but that little child acted like an angel. He came down here with her and he found out how he might be saved, and now that home is a little heaven. There is many a home that can be made happy.

The Little Greyhound in the Lion's Cage

A man over in Manchester had a little greyhound that he was training for a race, and he had a great bet on him for a poor man, and he was anxious his dog should succeed. The day came, and the dog didn't run at all. He was so mad that he took and beat the little greyhound, and then he pushed it through a cage in which there was a lion and expected to see it eaten, but the little dog ran right up to the lion as though it wanted mercy, and the lion, instead of eating it, began to lap it, and by-and-by the man called to the dog to come out, but he would not come.

Then he put his hand in, and the lion began to growl, and he took it out again. And some people went and told the keeper what the man had done and how he had ill-used the little greyhound. When the keeper came around, the man wanted him to get his dog out for him; and the keeper asked him how he got in there, and the man was ashamed to tell. At last the keeper said, "You put him in; you'd better go and get him out; I won't get him out for you." And so the dog has remained there ever since. Now, that may be a homely illustration, but I hope it will fasten on our minds the idea that we are no match for Satan. He has had six thousand years' experience. I always tremble when I hear a man talk about defying Satan, and I want to add "by the grace of God," for that is the only way. The lion of the tribe of Judah will take care of us if we will come to Him.

A Voice from the Tomb

The other day I read of a mother who died, leaving her child alone and very poor. She used to pray earnestly for her boy and left an impression upon his mind that she cared more for his soul than she cared for anything else in the world. He grew up to be a successful man in business and became very well off. One day, not long ago, after his mother had been dead for twenty years, he thought he would remove her remains, put her into his own lot in the cemetery, and put up a little monument to her memory. As he came to remove them and to lay them away, the thought came to him that while his mother was alive she had prayed for him, and he wondered why her prayers were not answered. That very night that man was saved. After his mother had been buried so long a time, the act of removing her body to another resting-place brought up all recollections of his childhood, and he became a Christian. Oh, you mothers!

DWIGHT L. MOODY

The Boy that went West

A number of years ago, before any railway came into Chicago, they used to bring in the grain from the western prairies in wagons for hundreds of miles, so as to have it shipped off by the lakes. There was a father who had a large farm out there, and who used to preach the gospel as well as to attend to his farm.

One day, when church business engaged him, he sent his son to Chicago with grain. He waited and waited for his boy to return, but he did not come home. At last he could wait no longer, so he saddled his horse and rode to the place where his son had sold the grain. He found that he had been there and got the money for his grain; then he began to fear that his boy had been murdered and robbed.

At last, with the aid of a detective, they tracked him to a gambling den, where they found that he had gambled away the whole of his money. In hopes of winning it back again, he then sold his team, and lost that money too. He had fallen among thieves, and, like the man who was going to Jericho, they stripped him, and then they cared no more about him.

What could he do? He was ashamed to go home to meet his father, and he fled. The father knew what it all meant. He knew the boy thought he would be very angry with him. He was grieved to think that his boy should have such feelings toward him.

That is just exactly like the sinner. He thinks because he has sinned, God will have nothing to do with him. But what did that father do? Did he say, "Let the boy go?" No; he went after him. He arranged his business and started after the boy. That man went from town to town, city to city. He would get the ministers to let him preach, and at the close he would tell his story. "I have got a boy who is a wanderer on the face of the earth somewhere." He would describe his boy, and say, "If you ever hear of him or see him, will you not write to me?" At last he found that he had gone to California, thousands of miles away. Did that father say, "Let him go?" No; off he went to the Pacific coast, seeking the boy. He went to San Francisco, and advertised in the newspapers that he would preach at such a church on such a day.

When he had preached, he told his story, in hopes that the boy might have seen the advertisement and come to the church. When he was done, away under the gallery, there was a young man who waited until the audience had gone out; then he came toward the pulpit. The father looked and saw it was that boy, and he ran to him and pressed him to his bosom. The boy wanted to confess what he had done, but not a word would the father hear. He forgave him freely and took him to his home once more.

I tell you Christ will welcome you this minute if you will come. Say, "I will arise and go to my Father." May God incline you to take this step. There is not one whom Jesus has not sought far longer than that father. There has not been a day since you left Him but He has followed you.

The Speaking Card

There was a friend of mine in Philadelphia going by a drinking saloon one night, and he saw in that saloon a professed Christian playing cards. He just took a pencil, wrote on a card, and saw a little boy and said, "My boy, here is some money. I want you to do an errand for me. You see that man on the side of the table where those three are playing cards with them?" Says he, "Yes, I do." "Well," says my friend, "just take that card to him."

The boy started, and my friend watched him when he handed this card to him. What was written on the card was, "Ye are my witnesses." The man took the card, looked at it, sprang to his feet, and rushing out into the street, asked the boy where the card came from. The boy said, "A man over there gave it to me." But the man had slipped away, and the poor man died a few months afterwards. "Ye are my witnesses." Wherever you find a professed Christian going in bad company, you may look for something worse.

The Imprisoned Children

When the Lawrence mills were on fire a number of years ago – I don't mean on fire, but when the mill fell in – the great mill fell in, and after it had fallen in, the ruins caught fire. There was only one room left entire, and in it three mission Sunday school children were imprisoned. The neighbors and all hands got their shovels and picks and crowbars, and were working to set the children free.

It came on night and they had not yet reached the children. When they were near them, by some mischance, a lantern broke, and the ruins caught fire. They tried to put it out but could not succeed. They could talk with the children, and even pass to them some coffee and refreshments, and encourage them to keep up. But, alas, the flames drew nearer and nearer to this prison. Superhuman were the efforts made to rescue the children; the men bravely fought back the flames; but the fire gained fresh strength and returned to claim its victims. Then, piercing shrieks arose when the spectators saw that the efforts of the firemen were hopeless.

The children saw their fate. They then knelt down and commenced to sing the little hymn we have all been taught in our Sunday school days, oh, how sweet, "Let others seek a home below which flames devour and waves overflow." The flames had now reached them; the stifling smoke began to pour into their little room, and they began to sink, one by one, upon the floor. A few moments more and the fire circled around them, and their souls were taken into the bosom of Christ. Yes, let others seek a home below if they will, but seek ye the kingdom of God with all your hearts.

Found in the Sand

While I was attending a meeting in a certain city some time ago, a lady came to me and said, "I want you to go home with me; I have something to say to you." When we reached her home, there were some friends there. After they had retired, she put her arms on the table, and tears began to come into her eyes, but with an effort she repressed her emotion.

After a struggle she went on to say that she was going to tell me something that she had never told any other living person. I should not tell it now, but she has gone to another world. She said she had a son in Chicago, and she was very anxious about him. When he was young he got interested in religion at the rooms of the Young Men's Christian Association. He used to go out in the street and circulate tracts. He was her only son, and she was very ambitious that he should make a name in the world and wanted him to get into the very highest circles.

Oh, what a mistake people make about these highest circles. Society is false; it is a sham. She was deceived like a good many more votaries of fashion and hunters after wealth at the present time. She thought it was beneath her son to go down and associate with those young men who hadn't much money. She tried to get him away from them, but they had more influence than she had; and, finally, to break his whole association, she packed him off to a boarding-school. He went soon to Yale College, and she supposed he got into one of those miserable secret societies there that have ruined so many young men, and the next thing she heard was that the boy had gone astray.

She began to write letters urging him to come into the kingdom of God; but she heard that he tore the letters up without reading them. She went to him to try and regain whatever influence she possessed over him, but her efforts were useless, and she came home with a broken heart. He left New Haven, and for two years they heard nothing of him. At last they heard he was in Chicago, and his father found him and gave him $30,000 to start in business. They thought it would change him, but it didn't.

They asked me, when I went back to Chicago, to try and use my influence with him. I got a friend to invite him to his house one night, where I intended to meet him, but he heard I was to be there and did not come near, like a good many other young men who seem to be afraid of me. I tried many times to reach him but could not. While I was traveling one day on the New Haven railroad, I bought a New York paper, and in it I saw a dispatch saying he had been drowned in Lake Michigan.

His father came on to find his body, and after considerable searching, they discovered it. All his clothes and his body were covered with sand. The body was taken home to that broken-hearted mother. She said, "If I thought he was in heaven I would have peace." Her disobedience of God's law came back upon her. So, my friends, if you have a boy impressed with the gospel, help him to come to Christ. Bring him in the arms of your faith, and He will unite you closer to Him.

Blind Bartimaeus

The apostle was going into Jericho for the last time. By the wayside he finds a poor, blind beggar who asks for a farthing, and he says, "Silver and gold have I none, but I can tell you of a great physician in Israel who can cure you."

"Can cure me?" he says. "I was born blind."

"Yes, but I have talked to a man in Jerusalem who says he was born blind, but now he sees."

"Why," says Bartimaeus, "how is that?"

"Well, sir, Jesus of Nazareth was in Jerusalem, and a boy, he said, led him up to Him, and He just made clay with spittle and anointed his eyes and sent him to wash in the pool of Siloam. If you could only go up to Jerusalem, all you would have do would be to tell Him. He don't charge anything."

"He don't charge anything?"

"No; He treats princes, potentates, and penniless all alike, for nothing; you have only to come before Him and ask Him."

I can see Bartimaeus' eyes light up as he cries out, "If I can get my eyes by asking, I will get them." He takes his place by the wayside in expectancy. All at once he hears someone coming, and he cries out, "Who is coming? What does it mean?"

At this no one answers him, but he begins to mistrust that it is Jesus of Nazareth. He has been told how great crowds flock about Him. And he cried out again in a louder voice, and they told him Jesus of Nazareth was passing by. And he cried again, then, with all his might, "Thou son of David, have mercy upon me."

Some in the crowd thought Christ was going up to Jerusalem to be crowned king and did not want Him to be disturbed by the blind beggar; they cried out not to disturb the Master, but the beggar would not cease, but cried all the louder, "Thou son of David, have mercy upon me."

And the prayer reached the ear of the Son of God, and he hushed all the voices about Him while He heard the earnest suitor. There was no mistake.

Higher and Higher

I remember a few years ago, a little child died, and just before his soul went home he asked his father to lift him up, and the father put his hand under the head of the child and raised it up. But the child only said, "That is not enough; that is not what I want; lift me right up." The child was wasted all to skin and bones, but still his father complied, and lifted the dying child out of his bed. But the little fellow kept whispering, fainter and fainter, "Lift me higher, higher, higher!"

And the father lifted higher and higher, till he lifted him as far as he could reach. Yet, still the barely audible whisper came, "Higher, father, higher," till at last, his head fell back, and his spirit passed up to the eternal King – high at last. So, my dear friends, let your constant cry be higher, higher, more near the cross of the Son of God.

Hold Up Your Light

Out west, a friend of mine was walking along one of the streets one dark night and saw approaching him a man with a lantern. As he came up close to him he noticed by the bright light that the man seemed as if he had no eyes. He went past; but the thought struck him, "Surely that man is blind." He turned around and said, "My friend, are you not blind?" "Yes." "Then what have you got the lantern for?" "I carry the lantern that people may not stumble over me, of course," said the man. Let us take a lesson from that blind man, and hold up our light, burning with the clear radiance of heaven, that men may not stumble over us.

The Horse that was Established

There was a little boy converted, and he was full of praise. When God converts boy or man his heart is full of joy; he can't help but praise God. His father was a professed Christian. The boy wondered why he didn't talk about Christ, and didn't go down to the special meetings. One day, as the father was reading the papers, the boy came to him and put his hand on his shoulder and said, "Why don't you praise God? Why don't you sing about Christ? Why don't you go down to these meetings that are being held?"

The father opened his eyes, and looked at him and said, gruffly, "I am not carried away with any of these doctrines. I am established." A few days after, they were getting out a load of wood. They put it on the cart. The father and the boy got on top of the load and tried to get the horse to go. They used the whip, but the horse wouldn't move. They got off and tried to roll the wagon along, but they could move neither the wagon nor the horse. "I wonder what's the matter?" said the father. "He's established," replied the boy. You may laugh at that, but this is the way with a good many Christians.

The Hand on Moody's Head

I remember when I was a boy, I went several miles from home with an older brother. That seemed to me the longest visit of my life. It seemed that I was then farther away from home than I had ever been before, or have ever been since. While we were walking down the street we saw an old man coming toward us, and my brother said, "There is a man that will give you a cent. He gives every new boy that comes into this town a cent." That was my first visit to the town, and when the old man got opposite to us he looked around, and my brother, not wishing me to lose the cent, and to remind the old man that I had not received it, told him that I was a new boy in the town. The old man, taking off my hat, placed his trembling hand on my head, and told me I had a Father in heaven.

It was a kind, simple act, but I feel the pressure of the old man's hand upon my head today. You don't know how much you may do by just speaking kindly.

The Idiot Boy

It is not long ago, it just seems the other day, when my dear friend Dr. Mathieson, now in heaven, told me he was preaching the gospel in Scotland and a minister told him he had in his congregation a little idiot boy. He did not know what to do with him; he had spoken to him many times, but the boy always said, "Ye maun wait till a' come to ye, and when a' come I'll sing ye a sang an' tell ye a story; but ye maun wait till a' come to ye."

The minister heard that the boy was dying, and he went to him and said, "Sandy, you promised me that you would sing me a song and tell me a story before you died; will you tell it now?"

"Yes, minister," replied the boy, "Three in ane an' ane in three, an' Jesus Christ He died for me; tha's a'" (Three in one and one in three, and Jesus Christ He died for me).

I tell you I would rather be a poor idiot, and know that, than be one of the mightiest and so-called wisest men in the city of Chicago, and not believe that Jesus took my place and died for me on Calvary's cross. The gospel is very simple; it is very easy to understand.

Believe

Have faith in God! Take Him at His word! Believe what He says! Believe the record God has given of His Son! I can imagine some of you saying, "I want to, but I have not got the right kind of faith."

What kind of faith do you want? Now, the idea that you want a different kind of faith is all wrong. Use the faith you have got, just believe on the Lord Jesus Christ.

Not only that, you can't give any reason for not believing. If a man told me he couldn't believe me, I should have a right to ask him why he couldn't believe me. I should have a right to ask him if I had ever broken my word with him; and if I had not broken my word with him, he ought to believe me. I would like to ask you, has God ever broken His word?

Never. My friends, He will keep His word. God condemns the world because they believe not on Him; that is the root of all evil.

A man who believes in the Lord Jesus Christ won't murder and lie and do all these awful things. Don't get caught up by that terrible delusion that unbelief is a misfortune. Unbelief is not a misfortune, but is the sin of the world. Christ found it on all sides of the world. When He first got up from the grave, He found that His disciples doubted. He had reason to cry out against unbelief.

The Bible

People say this Bible was good enough for ancient days, but we have men of culture, of science, of literature now, and its value has decreased to the people of our day. Now, give me a better book, and I will throw it away. Has the world ever offered us a better book? These men want us to give up the Bible. What are you going to give us in its place? Oh, how cruel infidelity is to tell us to give up all the hope we have, to throw away the only book which tells the story of the resurrection. They try to tell us that it is all a fiction, so that when we lay our loved ones in the grave, we bid them farewell for time and eternity. Away with this terrible doctrine! The Bible of our fathers and mothers is true, and the good old way is true.

When man comes and tries to draw us from the old to the new way, it is the work of the devil. But men say we have outgrown this way. Why don't men outgrow the light of the sun? They shouldn't let the light of the sun come into their buildings, they should have gas – the sun is old, and gas is a new light. There is just as much sense in this as to take away the Bible.

How much we owe the blessed Bible! Why, I don't think human life would be safe if it wasn't for it. Look at the history of the nations where the Bible has been trampled underfoot. Only a few years ago France and England were nearly equal. England threw the Bible open to the world, and France tried to trample it. Now, the English language is spoken around the world, and its prosperity has increased, while England stands foremost among the nations. But look at France. It has gone down and down with anarchy and revolution. Let us not forsake the old way.

Willie

I said to my little family, one morning, a few weeks before the Chicago fire, "I am coming home this afternoon to give you a ride."

My little boy clapped his hands. "Oh papa, will you take me to see the bears in Lincoln park?"

"Yes." You know boys are very fond of seeing bears. I had not been gone long when my little boy said, "Mamma, I wish you would get me ready."

"O," she said, "it will be a long time before your papa comes."

"But I want to get ready, mamma." At last he was ready to have the ride, face washed and clothes all nice and clean.

"Now, you must take good care and not get yourself dirty again," said mamma. Oh, of course he was going to take care; he wasn't going to get dirty. So off he ran to watch for me.

However, it was a long time yet until the afternoon, and after a little he began to play. When I got home, I found him outside, with his face all covered with dirt.

"I can't take you to the park that way, Willie."

"Why, papa, you said you would take me."

"Ah, but I can't; you're all over mud. I couldn't be seen with such a dirty little boy."

"Why, I's clean, papa; mamma washed me."

"Well, you've got dirty since."

But he began to cry, and I could not convince him that he was dirty. "I's clean; mamma washed me!" he cried. Do you think I argued with him? No. I just took him up in my arms, and carried him into the house, and showed him his face in the looking-glass. He had not a word to say. He could not take my word for it; but one look at the glass was enough; he saw it for himself. He didn't say he wasn't dirty after that!

Now, the looking-glass showed him that his face was dirty, *but I did not take the looking-glass to wash it;* of course not. Yet that is just what thousands of people do. The law is the looking-glass to see ourselves in, to show us how vile and worthless we are in the sight of God; but they take the law and try to *wash* themselves with it.

Two Boys and Two Fathers

Whenever I think about this subject, two fathers come before me. One lived on the Mississippi river. He was a man of great wealth. Yet he would have freely given it all, could he have brought back his eldest boy from his early grave.

One day that boy had been borne home unconscious. They did everything that man could do to restore him, but in vain.

"He must die," said the doctor.

"But, doctor," said the agonized father, "can you do nothing to bring him to consciousness, even for a moment?"

"That may be," said the doctor, "but he can never live."

Time passed, and after a terrible suspense, the father's wish was gratified. "My son," he whispered, "the doctor tells me you are dying."

"Well," said the boy, "you never prayed for me, father; won't you pray for my lost soul now?" The father wept. It was true, he had never prayed. He was a stranger to God. And in a little while that soul, unprayed for, passed into its dark eternity.

Oh father, if your boy was dying, and he called on you to pray, could you lift your burdened heart to heaven? Have you learned this sweetest lesson of heaven on earth, to know and hold communion with your God? And before this evil world has marked your dearest treasures for its prey, have you learned to lead your little ones to a children's Christ?

What a contrast is the other father! He, too, had a lovely boy, and one day he came home to find him at the gates of death.

"A great change has come over our boy," said the weeping mother; "he has only been a little ill before, but it seems now as if he were dying fast." The father went into the room and placed his hand on the forehead of the little boy. He could see the boy was dying. He could feel the cold damp of death.

"My son, do you know you are dying?"

"No; am I?"

"Yes; you are dying."

"And shall I die today?"

"Yes, my boy, you cannot live till night."

"Well, then, I shall be with Jesus tonight, won't I, father?"

"Yes, my son, you will spend tonight with the Savior."

Mothers and fathers, the little ones may begin early; be in earnest with them now. You know not how soon you may be taken from them, or they may be taken from you. Therefore let this impression be made upon their minds, that you care for their souls a million times more than for their worldly prospects.

Little Great Men

One afternoon I noticed a lady at the services whom I knew to be a Sunday school teacher. After the service I asked her where her class was. "O," said she, "I went to the school and found only a little boy, and so I came away."

"Only a little boy!" said I. "Think of the value of one such soul! The fires of a reformation may be slumbering in that tow-headed boy; there may be a young Knox, or a Wesley, or a Whitefield in your class."

The Demoniac

When this man found himself delivered, he wanted to go with the Savior. That was gratitude. Christ had saved him and redeemed him. He had redeemed him from the hand of the enemy.

And this man cried, "Let me follow you around the world; where You go I will go."

But the Lord said, "You go home and tell your friends what good things the Lord has done for you."

And he started home. I would like to have been in that house when he came there. I can imagine how the children would look when they saw him, and say, "Father is coming."

"Shut the door," the mother would cry. "Lookout! fasten the window; bolt every door in the house." Many times, he very likely had come and abused his family, and broken the chairs and tables and turned the mother into the street and alarmed all the neighbors.

They see him now coming down the street. Down he comes till he gets to the door, and then gently knocks. You don't hear a sound as he stands there. At last he sees his wife at the window and he says, "Mary!"

"Why," she says, "he speaks as he did when I first married him; I wonder if he has got well?" So she looks out and asks, "John, is that you?"

"Yes, Mary," he replies, "it's me; don't be afraid anymore; I'm well now." I see that mother, how she pulls back the bolts of that door and looks at him. The first look is sufficient, and she springs into his arms and clings about his neck. She takes him in and asks him a hundred questions – how it all happened – all about it.

"Well, just take a chair and I'll tell you how I got cured." The children hang back and look amazed. He says, "I was there in the tombs, you know, cutting myself with stones, and running about in my nakedness, when Jesus of Nazareth came that way. Mary, did you ever hear of Him? He is the most wonderful man; I've never seen a man like Him. He just ran in and told those devils to leave me, and they left me. When He had cured me, I wanted to follow Him. But He told me to come home and tell you all about it."

The children by-and-by gathered about his knee, and the elder ones ran to tell their playmates what wonderful things Jesus had done for their father. Ah, my friends, we have got a mighty deliverer; I don't care what affliction you have, He will deliver you from it.

A Good Mother

A young man went home from one of our meetings some time ago. He had been converted. He had previously been a dissipated young man. His mother had made it a rule, she told me, that she "would not retire till he came home." That was her rule, she said, "never to go to bed till my boy was at home. If he did not come home till five o'clock in the morning, I sat up, and when he was out all night I got no sleep; but when he came home I always met him with a kiss.

"I threw my arms around his neck. I treated him just as if he was kind, attentive, and good. Sometimes he would be out all night. Those nights I would not go to bed. He used to know it. One night he came home. I looked to see if he was under the influence of liquor. He came up to me, and he said, 'Mother, I have been converted,' and then I fell on his neck and embraced him, and wept over him tears of joy.

"Why," said she, "Mr. Moody, you don't know what joy it

gave me. I cannot tell you. You don't know what a load it took off my heart. You don't know how I praised God that my prayers had been answered."

In Jail

I remember a mother who heard that her boy was impressed at one of our meetings. She said her son was a good enough boy, and he didn't need to be converted. I pleaded with that mother, but all my pleading was of no account. I tried my influence with the boy; but when I was pulling one way she was pulling the other, and of course her influence prevailed. Naturally it would.

Well, to make a long story short, some time after, I happened to be in the county jail, and I saw him there. "How did you come here?" I asked. "Does your mother know where you are?"

"No, don't tell her; I came in under an assumed name, and I am going to Joliet for four years. Do not let my mother know this," he pleaded; "she thinks I am in the army."

I used to call on that mother, but I had promised her boy I would not tell her, and for four years she mourned over that boy. She thought he had died on the battle-field or in a southern hospital. What a blessing he might have been to that mother, if she had only helped us to bring him to Christ!

The Repentant Son

I remember to have heard a story of a bad boy who had run away from home. He had given his father no end of trouble. He had refused all the invitations which his father had sent him to come home and be forgiven and help comfort his old heart. He had even gone so far as to scoff at his father and mother.

But one day a letter came, telling him his father was dead, and they wanted him to come home and attend the funeral. At first, he determined he would not go, but then he thought it would be a shame not to pay some little respect to the memory of so good a man; and so, just as a matter of form, he took the train and went to the old home, sat through all the funeral services, saw his father buried, and came back with the rest of the friends to the house, with his heart as cold and stony as ever.

But when the old man's will was brought out to be read, the ungrateful son found that his father had remembered him along with the rest of the family, and had left him an inheritance with the others who had not gone astray. This broke his heart in penitence. It was too much for him, and his old father, during all those years in which he had been so wicked and rebellious, had never ceased to love him.

That is just the way our Father in Heaven does with us. That is just the way Jesus does with people who refuse to give their hearts to Him. He loves them in spite of their sins, and it is this love which, more than anything else, brings hard-hearted sinners to their knees.

The Prodigal's Return

I can see him now. He has resolved. His old associates laugh at him, but what does he care for public opinion? "I have made up my mind," he says. He doesn't stay to get a new suit of clothes, as some men do in coming to Christ. They want to do some good deeds before they come. He just started as he was.

I see him walking on through dusty roads and over hills, and fording brooks and rivers. It didn't take him long to go home when he made up his mind. Then the prodigal is nearing the homestead; see him.

I remember going home after being away for a few months. How I longed to catch a glimpse of that old place! As I neared it, I remembered the sweet hours I had spent with my brother, and the pleasant days of childhood.

Here is the prodigal as he comes near his old home; all his days of happy childhood come before him. He wonders if the old man is still alive, and as he comes near the home he says, "It may be that the old man is dead." Ah, what a sad thing it would have been if on returning he had found that his father had gone down to his grave mourning for him. Is there any one here who has a father and mother whose love you are scorning, and to whom you have not written for years?

I said to a prodigal the other night, "How long is it since you have written to your mother?"

"Four years and a half."

"Don't you believe your mother loves you?" "Yes," he replied, "it is because she does love me that I don't write to her. If I was telling her the life I've been leading, it would break her heart."

"If you love her," I said, "go and write her tonight and tell her all."

I got his promise, and I am happy. I can't tell how glad I feel when I get those young prodigals to turn to their fathers and mothers, because I know what joy will be in the hearts of those parents when they hear from their prodigal son.

As he nears his father's home, he wonders again if his heart has turned against him, or if he will receive a welcome. Ah, he doesn't know his father's heart.

I can see the old man up there on that flat roof, in the cool of the day, waiting for his boy. Every day he has been there, every day straining his eyes over the country to catch the first glimpse of his son should he return.

This evening he is there, still hoping to see the wanderer come back. By-and-by he sees a form in the distance coming toward the house. As he comes nearer and nearer, he can tell it is the form of a young man. He cannot tell who it is by his dress. His robe is gone, his ring is gone, his shoes are gone, but the old man catches sight of the face.

I see him as he comes running down, as if the spirit of youth has come upon him, his long white hair floating through the air. He rushes past his servants, out the door, and up to his son, whom he takes to his bosom. He rejoices over him. The young man tries to make a speech; tries to ask him to be one of his servants, but the father won't listen to it. When he gets him to the house he cries to one servant, "Go, get the best robe for him"; to another, "You go and get a ring and put on his finger"; "Get shoes for him," he cries to another; "Go, kill the fatted calf," is the order given to another, "for my son has returned."

Ah, there was joy there. "My boy who was dead is alive again." There was joy in that house.

Very Sad News

I know a mother who lives down in the southern part of Indiana. Some years ago, her boy came up to Chicago. He hadn't been in the city long before he was led astray. A neighbor happened to come up to Chicago and found him one night in the streets drunk.

When that neighbor went home, at first he thought he wouldn't say anything about it to the boy's father, but afterwards he thought it his duty to tell him. So, in a crowd in the street of their little town, he just took the father aside and told him what he had seen in Chicago. It was a terrible blow.

When the children had been put to bed that night he said to his wife, "Wife, I have bad news. I have heard from Chicago today."

The mother dropped her work in an instant and said, "Tell me what it is."

"Well, our son has been seen on the streets of Chicago, drunk."

Neither of them slept that night, but they took their burden to Christ, and about daylight the mother said, "I don't know how, when or where, but God has given me faith to believe that our son will be saved and will never come to a drunkard's grave."

One week after, the boy left Chicago. He couldn't tell why; an unseen power seemed to lead him to his mother's home, and the first thing he said on coming over the threshold was,

"Mother, I have come home to ask you to pray for me." And soon after he came back to Chicago a bright and shining light.

The Little Orphan's Prayer

A little child whose father and mother had died, was taken into another family. The first night she asked if she could pray, as she used to do. They said, "Oh, yes."

So, she knelt down and prayed as her mother taught her; and when that was ended she added a little prayer of her own, "Oh God, make these people as kind to me as father and mother were." Then she paused and looked up, as if expecting the answer, and added, "Of course He will." How sweetly simple was that little one's faith; she expected God to "do," and of course, she got her request.

The Child Angel

I remember a number of years ago I went out of Chicago to try to preach. I went down to a little town where was being held a Sunday school convention. I was a perfect stranger in the place, and when I arrived, a man stepped up to me and asked me if my name was Moody. I told him it was, and he invited me to his house.

When I got there, he said he had to go to the convention, and asked me to excuse his wife, as she, not having a servant, had to attend to her household duties. He put me into the parlor and told me to amuse myself as best I could till he came back.

I sat there, but the room was dark, and I could not read, and I got tired. So, I thought I would try and get the children and play with them. I listened for some sound of children in the house, but could not hear a single evidence of the presence of little ones.

When my friend came back I said, "Haven't you any children?"

"Yes," he replied, "I have one, but she's in heaven, and I am glad she is there, Moody."

"Are you glad that your child's dead?" I inquired.

He went on to tell me how he had worshiped that child; how his whole life had been bound up in her to the neglect of his Savior.

One day he had come home and found her dying. Upon her death he accused God of being unjust. He saw some of his neighbors with their children around them. Why hadn't He taken some of them away? He was rebellious.

After he came home from her funeral he said, "All at once I thought I heard her little voice calling me, but the truth came to my heart that she was gone. Then I thought I heard her feet upon the stairs; but I knew she was lying in the grave. The thought of her loss almost made me mad. I threw myself on my bed and wept bitterly. I fell asleep, and while I slept I had a dream, but it almost seemed to me like a vision.

"I thought I was going over a barren field, and I came to a river so dark and chill-looking that I was going to turn away, when all at once I saw on the opposite bank the most beautiful sight I ever looked at. I thought death and sorrow could never enter into that lovely region.

Then I began to see beings all so happy looking, and among

them I saw my little child. She waved her little angel hand to me and cried, 'Father, father, come this way.'

I thought her voice sounded much sweeter than it did on earth. In my dream I thought I went to the water and tried to cross it, but found it deep, and the current so rapid that I thought if I entered, it would carry me away from her forever. I tried to find a boatman to take me over, but couldn't, and I walked up and down the river trying to find a crossing, and still she cried, 'Come this way.'

All at once I heard a voice come rolling down, 'I am the way, the truth and the life; no man cometh unto the Father but by Me.' The voice awoke me from my sleep, and I knew it was my Savior calling me, and pointing the way for me to reach my darling child. I am now superintendent of a Sunday school; I have made many converts; my wife has been converted, and we will, through Jesus as the way, see one day our child."

Rover

I remember when Dr. Arnold, who has gone to God, was delivering a sermon; he used this illustration. The sermon and text have all gone, but that illustration is fresh upon my mind to-night and brings home the truth.

He said, "You have been sometimes out at dinner with a friend, and you have seen the faithful household dog standing watching every mouthful his master takes. All the crumbs that fall on the floor he picks up, and seems eager for them, but when his master takes a plate of beef and puts it on the floor and says, 'Rover, here's something for you,' he comes up and smells of it, looks at his master, and goes away to a corner of the room.

He was willing to eat the crumbs, but he wouldn't touch the roast beef; thought it was too good for him." That is the way with a good many Christians. They are willing to eat the crumbs, but not willing to take all God wants. Come boldly to the throne of grace and get the help you need; there is an abundance for every man, woman and child.

Faith

I remember a child that lived with her parents in a small village. One day the news came that her father had joined the army (it was at the beginning of our war), and a few days after, the landlord came to demand the rent. The mother told him she hadn't got it, and that her husband had gone into the army.

He was a hardhearted wretch, and he stormed and said that they must leave the house; he wasn't going to have people who couldn't pay the rent. After he was gone, the mother threw herself into the arm-chair and began to weep bitterly. Her little girl, whom she had taught to pray in faith (but it is more difficult to practice than to preach), came up to her and said, "What makes you cry, mamma? I will pray to God to give us a little house, and won't He?"

What could the mother say? So, the little child went into the next room and began to pray. The door was open, and the mother could hear every word, "Oh God, you have come and taken away father, and mamma has got no money, and the landlord will turn us out because we can't pay, and we will have to sit on the doorstep, and mamma will catch cold. Give us a little home."

Then she waited as if for an answer, and then added, "Won't you, please, God?" She came out of the room quite happy, expecting a house to be given them. The mother felt reproved. I can tell you, however, she has never paid any rent since, for God heard the prayer of that little one and touched the heart of the cruel landlord. God give us the faith of that little child, that we may likewise expect an answer, "nothing wavering."

Son, Remember

I have been twice in the jaws of death. Once I was drowning, and the third time I was about to sink, I was rescued. In the twinkling of an eye everything I had said, done, or thought of, flashed across my mind. I do not understand how everything in a man's life can be crowded into his recollection in an instant of time, but nevertheless it all flashed through my mind.

Another time when I thought I was dying, it all came back to me again. It is just so that all things we think we have forgotten will come back by-and-by; it is only a question of time. We will hear the words, "Son, remember," and it is a good deal better for us now to remember our sins and confess them before it is too late.

Christ said to His disciples, "Remember Lot's wife." Over and over again, when the children of Israel were brought out of Egypt, God said to them, "Remember where I found you, and how I delivered you." He wanted them to remember His goodness to them, and the time is coming when, if they forget His goodness and despise it, they will be without mercy.

Reaping the Whirlwind

I remember in the north of England a prominent citizen told a sad case that happened there in the city of Newcastle-on-Tyne. It was about a young boy. He was very young. He was an only child. The father and mother thought everything of him and did all they could for him.

But he fell into bad ways. He took up with evil characters, and finally got to running with thieves. He didn't let his parents know about it. By-and-by the gang he was with broke into the house, and he with them. Yes, he had to do it all. They stopped outside of the building, while he crept in and started to rob the till.

He was caught in the act, taken into court, tried, convicted, and sent to the penitentiary for ten years. He worked on and on in the convict's cell, till at last his term was out, and at once started for home.

And when he came back to the town, he started down the street where his father and mother used to live. He went to the house and rapped. A stranger came to the door and stared him in the face. "No, there's no such person lives here, and where your parents are I don't know," was the only welcome he received.

Then he turned through the gate and down the street, asking even the children that he met about his folks, where they were living, and if they were well. But everybody looked blank. Ten years rolled by, and though that seemed perhaps a short time, how many changes had taken place!

There where he was born and brought up, he was now an alien and unknown, even in the old haunts. But at last he found a couple of townsmen that remembered his father and mother, but they told him the old house had been deserted long years ago, that he had been gone but a few months before his father was confined to his house and very soon after died broken-hearted, and that his mother had gone out of her mind.

He went up to the mad-house where his mother was and went up to her and said, "Mother, mother, don't you know me? I am your son." But she raved and slapped him on the face and shrieked, "You are not my son," and then raved again and tore her hair.

He left the asylum more dead than alive, so completely broken-hearted that he died in a few months. Yes, the fruit was long growing, but at the last it ripened on the harvest like a whirlwind.

The Praying Little Cripple

I once knew a little cripple who lay upon her death-bed. She had given herself to God and was distressed only because she could not labor for Him actively among the lost.

Her clergyman visited her, and hearing her complaint, told her that there from her sick-bed she could offer prayers for those whom she wished to see turning to God. He advised her to write the names down, and then to pray earnestly; and then he went away and thought of the subject no more.

Soon a feeling of great religious interest sprang up in the village, and the churches were crowded nightly. The little cripple heard of the progress of the revival and inquired anxiously for the names of the saved.

A few weeks later she died, and among a roll of papers that was found under her little pillow was one bearing the names of fifty-six persons, every one of whom had in the revival been converted. By each name was a little cross, by which the poor, crippled saint had checked off the name of the converts as they had been reported to her.

A Boy's Victory

I remember when out in Kansas, while holding a meeting, I saw a little boy who came up to the window crying. I went to him and said, "My little boy, what is your trouble?"

"Why, Mr. Moody, my mother's dead, and my father drinks, and they don't love me, and the Lord won't have anything to do with me because I am a poor drunkard's boy."

"You have got a wrong idea, my boy; Jesus will love you and save you, and your father too," and I told him a story of a little boy in an eastern city.

The boy said his father would never allow the canting hypocrites of Christians to come into his house, and would never allow his child to go to Sunday school. A kind-hearted man got his little boy and brought him to Christ. When Christ gets into a man's heart, he cannot help but pray.

This father had been drinking one day and coming home he heard that boy praying. He went to him and said, "I don't want you to pray any more. You've been along with some of those Christians. If I catch you praying again I'll flog you." But the boy was filled with God, and he couldn't help praying.

The door of communication was opened between him and Christ, and his father caught him praying again. He went to him. "Didn't I tell you never to pray again? If I catch you at it once more, you leave my house." He thought he would stop him.

Not very long after this, one day, his father had been drinking more than usual, and coming in found the boy offering a prayer. He caught the boy with a push and said, "Didn't I tell you never to pray again? Leave this house. Get your things packed up and go."

The little fellow hadn't many things to get together – a drunkard's boy never has – and he went up to his mother's room. "Good-bye, mother."

"Where are you going?"

"I don't know where I'll go, but father says I cannot stay here any longer; I've been praying again," he said.

The mother knew it wouldn't do to try to keep the boy when her husband had ordered him away, so she drew him to her bosom and kissed him and bid him good-bye. He went to his brothers and sisters and kissed them good-bye.

When he came to the door, his father was there, and the little fellow reached out his hand. "Good-bye, father; as long as I live I will pray for you," and left the house. He hadn't been gone many minutes when the father rushed after him.

"My boy, if that is religion, if it can drive you away from father and mother and home, I want it." Yes, maybe some other little boy has got a drinking father and mother. Lift your voice to heaven, and the news will be carried up to heaven, "He prays."

The Young Converts

There are four men coming down the streets of Capernaum. I never knew them, but if I met them in the streets of Boston, I should feel like grasping them by the hand.

Perhaps one of them was he who was converted not long before; perhaps the other was the leper who went to Jesus and got cured, and when he came home, his wife didn't know who it was, and couldn't believe it was her husband; and another had been cured perhaps of blindness, and here was the man with the palsy who had nearly shaken himself into his grave.

The doctors of Jerusalem had all given him up as a hopeless case. "Why," they said, "he cannot even get his food to his mouth, he shakes so. We can't do anything with him."

Well, these young converts came along – I suppose they were young; they have more faith than anyone else – and they see this man with the palsy and instantly say that one word from Him will put it away.

But they cannot get him there; they don't see how they can carry him, and finally one of them goes and gets a neighbor, and says, "Here's a man with the palsy; if we can get him up to where Christ is, He can just heal him at once."

I think he would be astonished, and say, "What, save that man; impossible! He can't be cured."

But the young convert persists, and tells him of those who had been made to see, and the deaf to hear, and the lame to walk, and so convinced the neighbor that at last he said, "Well,

I will help you and go and see this wonderful physician," and away they go and hunt up another young convert, who had been lame for years.

He is not strong enough to help them, however, and they find another man. He has been deaf and dumb for years. And these four young converts take this man with the palsy and put him, I suppose, on what we called during the war a stretcher, and away they go to Christ.

They had faith in what they were about. I can imagine the young men saying, as they carry him along, "We will not have to carry him back again; the palsy will be gone; it will be cured then."

On they go with their load, and when they get to the house, they find it crowded inside and a multitude standing outside. They say to the people, "Let us pass; we want to take the poor man to Christ."

But they say, "Why, there is no hope for him; he is past all cure."

"Ah," say the young converts, "that is nothing. Jesus of Nazareth can cure him; all things are possible to Him."

But they wouldn't stand aside. They wouldn't allow them to get in. But these four men are not going to take this man back. They are determined not to fail. They hesitate a moment, then go to the next house; it is a neighbor's. There were no bells in those days, and so they knock.

When the neighbor comes to the door they say, "We want to get into the next house; let us go through yours."

"Oh, yes," says the man, and they ascend the staircase and get on the roof and get over to the next house. There's no entrance through there, and so they dig a hole, they tear up this roof. A great many people in this city would be opposed to this sort of thing. They would say, "If you want to get into the house, you want things to be done decently; don't tear up the roof in that way." But, my friends, if we want to go to work for Christ, we must tear off the top of the house, if it's necessary. We must use vigorous means.

These young men had good faith, and that's what we want here. But when they had torn off the roof they had nothing to let the man down by. So, they looked about and made a rope of their own clothing, and down they laid him right among the Pharisees and learned doctors, right at the feet of Jesus.

And it is a good place to put a poor sinner. And we are not told whether that man with the palsy had any faith. But the Son of God looked up and saw their faith, the faith of the four men, and it pleased Him. It was like a cup of refreshment that satisfied the longings of His soul; He saw the brightness of their faith when He looked upon them. And He said to the sick man, "Son, be of good cheer, thy sins are forgiven thee."

Lost on the Deep

I read some time ago of a vessel that had been off on a whaling voyage and had been gone about three years. I saw the account in print somewhere lately, but it happened a long time ago.

The father of one of those sailors had charge of the lighthouse, and he was expecting his boy to come home. It was time for the whaling vessel to return.

One night there came up a terrible gale, and this father fell asleep, and while he slept his light went out. When he awoke, he looked toward the shore and saw there had been a vessel wrecked. He at once went to see if he could not yet save someone who might be still alive.

The first body that came floating towards the shore was, to his great grief and surprise, the body of his own boy. He had been watching for that boy for many days, and he had been gone for three years. Now, the boy had at last come in sight of home, and had perished because his father had let his light go out. I thought, what an illustration of fathers and mothers today that have let their light go out!

Looking Down from Heaven

I remember in the exposition building in Dublin, while I was speaking about heaven, I said something to the effect that, "perhaps at this moment a mother is looking down from heaven upon her daughter here tonight," and I pointed down to a young lady in the audience. Next morning, I received this letter:

"On Wednesday, when you were speaking of heaven, you said, 'It may be this moment there is a mother looking down from heaven expecting the salvation of her child who is here.' You were apparently looking at the very spot where my child was sitting. My heart said, 'That is *my* child. That is *her* mother.'

Tears sprang to my eyes. I bowed my head and prayed, 'Lord, direct that word to my darling child's heart; Lord, save my child.' I was then anxious till the close of the meeting, when I went to her. She was bathed in tears. She rose, put her arms round me, and kissed me.

When walking down to you she told me it was that same remark (about the mother looking down from heaven) that found the way home to her, and she asked me, 'Papa, what can I do for Jesus?'"

Sunday School Love

In Chicago a few years ago, there was a little boy who went to one of the mission Sunday schools. His father moved to another part of the city about five miles away, and every Sunday that boy came past thirty or forty Sunday schools to the one he attended.

And one Sunday, a lady who was out collecting scholars for a Sunday school met him and asked why he went so far, past so many schools. "There are plenty of others," said she, "just as good."

He said, "They may be as good, but they are not so good for me."

"Why not?" she asked.

"Because they love a fellow over there," he answered. Ah, love won him! "Because they love a fellow over there!" How easy it is to reach people through love!"

Sunday school teachers should win the affections of their scholars if they wish to lead them to Christ.

The Little Norwegian Boy

I remember while in Boston I attended one of the daily prayer-meetings. The meetings we had been holding had been almost always addressed by young men.

Well, in that meeting, a little tow-headed Norwegian boy stood up. He could hardly speak a word of English plain, but he got up and came to the front. He trembled all over, and the tears were trickling down his cheeks, but he spoke out as well as he could, and said, "If I tell the world about Jesus, then will He tell the Father about me."

He then took his seat; that was all he said; but I tell you that in those few words he said more than all of them, old and young together. Those few words went straight down into the heart of every one present. "If I tell the world;" yes, that's what it means to confess Christ.

Hold the Fort

I am told that when General Sherman went through Atlanta toward the sea, through the southern states; he left in the fort, in the Kennesaw mountains, a little handful of men to guard some rations that he brought there.

And General Hood got into the outer rear and attacked the fort, drove the men in from the outer works into the inner works, and for a long time the battle raged fearfully. Half of the men were either killed or wounded; the general who was in command was wounded seven different times; and when they were about ready to run up the white flag and surrender the fort, Sherman got within fifteen miles, and through the signal corps on the mountain he sent the message, "Hold the fort; I am coming. W. T. Sherman." That message fired up their hearts, and they held the fort till reinforcements came, and the fort did not go into the hands of their enemies.

Our friend, Mr. Bliss, has written a hymn entitled "Hold the fort, for I am coming," and I'm going to ask Mr. Sankey to sing that hymn. I hope there will be a thousand young converts coming into our ranks to help hold the fort. Our Savior is in command, and He is coming. Let us take up the chorus.

> Ho! my comrades, see the signal.
> > Waving in the sky!
> Reinforcements now appearing,
> > Victory is nigh!
>
> CHO. – "Hold the fort, for I am coming,"
> > Jesus signals still,
> Wave the answer back to heaven,
> > "By Thy grace we will."
>
> See the mighty hosts advancing,
> > Satan lending on;
> Mighty men around us falling,
> > Courage almost gone. – CHO .

See the glorious banner waving,
    Hear the bugle blow,
In our leader's name we'll triumph
    Over every foe. – CHO.

Fierce and long the battle rages,
    But our Help is near;
Onward comes our Great Commander,
    Cheer, my comrades, cheer! – CHO.
        -P. P. Bliss.

The Collier and His Children

When I was holding meetings a little time ago, at Wharncliff, in England, a coal district, a great burly collier came up to me, and said in his Yorkshire dialect, "Dost know wha was at meetin' t'night?"

"No," I answered.

"Why," said he, "So-and-so" (mentioning name). The name was a familiar one. He was a very bad man, one of the wildest, wickedest men in Yorkshire according to his own confession, and according to the confession of everybody who knew him.

"Well," said the man, "he cam' into meetin' an' said you didn't preach right; he said thou didn't preach nothin' but the love o' Christ, an' that won't do for drunken colliers; ye want shake 'em over a pit, and he says he'll ne'er come again."

He thought I didn't preach about hell. Mark you, my friends, I believe in the pit that burns, in the fire that's never quenched, in the worm that never dies; but I believe that the magnet that goes down to the bottom of the pit is the love of Jesus. I didn't expect to see him again, but he came the next night, without washing his face, right from the pit, with all his working clothes upon him.

This drunken collier sat down on one of the seats that were used for the children and got as near to me as possible. The sermon was love from first to last. He listened at first attentively, but by-and-by I saw him with the sleeve of his rough coat, wiping his eyes.

Soon after we had an inquiry-meeting, when some of those praying colliers got around him, and it wasn't long before he was crying, "Oh Lord, save me; I am lost; Jesus, have mercy upon me"; and he left that meeting a new creature.

His wife told me herself what occurred when he came home. His little children heard him coming along; they knew the step of his heavy clogs, and ran to their mother in terror, clinging to her skirts. He opened the door as gently as could be. He had a habit of banging the doors.

When he came into the house and saw the children clinging to their mother, frightened, he just stooped down and picked up the youngest girl in his arms and looked at her, the tears rolling down his cheeks. "Mary, God has sent thy father home to thee," and kissed her. He picked up another, "God has sent thy father home"; and from one to another he went and kissed them all; and then came to his wife and put his arms around her neck, "Don't cry, lass; don't cry. God has sent thy husband home at last; don't cry," and all she could do was to put her arms around his neck and sob.

And then he said, "Have you got a Bible in the house, lass?"

They hadn't such a thing. "Well, lass, if we haven't we must pray." They got down on their knees, and all he could say was:

> "Gentle Jesus, meek and mild,
>   Look upon a little child;
> Pity my simplicity –
>   for Jesus Christ's sake, amen."

It was a simple prayer, but God answered it. While I was at Barnet some time after that, a friend came to me, and said, "I've got good news for you. So-and-so [mentioning the collier s name] is preaching the gospel everywhere he goes, in the pit and out of the pit, and tries to win everybody to the Lord Jesus Christ."

Young Moody's Conversion

Let me give you a leaf out of my experience. When I was in Boston, I used to attend a Sabbath school class, and one day I recollect a Sabbath school teacher came around behind the counter of the shop I used to work in, and put his hand on my shoulder, and talked to me about Christ and my soul.

I had not felt I had a soul till then. I said, "This is a very strange thing; here is a man who never saw me till within a few days, and he is weeping over my sins, and I never shed a tear about them." But I understand it now and know what it is to have a passion for men's souls and weep over their sins.

I don't remember what he said, but I can feel the power of that young man's hand on my shoulder tonight. Young Christian men, go and lay your hand on your comrade's shoulder, and point him to Jesus.

Well, he got me up to the school, and it was not long before I was brought into the kingdom of God. I went thousands of miles away after that, but I often thought I should like to see that man again.

Time rolled on, and at length I was at Boston again; and I recollect, one night when I was preaching there, a fine, noble-looking young man came up the aisle, and said, "I should like to speak with you, Mr. Moody; I have often heard my father talk about you."

"Who is your father?" I asked. "Edward Kemble," was the reply.

"What!" said I, "my old Sunday school teacher?" I asked him his name, and he said it was Henry, and that he was seventeen years of age.

I tried to put my hand on his shoulder just where his father did on my shoulder, and I said to him, "You are just as old as I was when your father put his hand on my shoulder. Are you a Christian, Henry?"

"No, sir," he said; and as I talked to him about his soul with my hand on his shoulder, the tears began to trickle down.

"Come," said I, "I will show you how you can be saved," and I took him into a pew and quoted promise after promise to him. And I went on praying with him, but as he did not get light, I read to him the fifty-third chapter of Isaiah, "'All we, like sheep, have gone astray.' Do you believe that, Henry?"

"Yes, sir, I know that's true."

"'We have turned every one to his own way.' Is that true?"

"Yes, sir; that's true, and that's what troubles me; I like my own way."

"But there is another sentence yet, Henry; 'The Lord hath laid on Him the iniquity of us all.' Do you believe that, Henry?"

"No, I do not, sir."

"Now," I said, "why should you take a verse of God's word and cut it in two and believe one part and not another. Here are two things against you, and you believe them; and here is one in your favor, but you won't believe that. What authority have you for serving God's word in that way?"

"Well," he said, "Mr. Moody, if I believed *that* I should be saved."

"I know you would," I replied, "and that's exactly what I want you to do. But you take the bitter and won't have the sweet with it." So, I held him to that little word *hath* – "He *hath* laid on Him the iniquity of us all."

A Little Child Shall Lead Them

A little child at one of the meetings was seen talking so earnestly to a companion that a lady sat by her to hear what she was saying, and found that the dear child was telling how much Jesus loved her, and how she loved Him, and asked her little companion if she would not love Him too.

The lady was so much impressed by the child's words that she spoke to an anxious soul that very night for the first time in her life. And so "a little child shall lead them."

A Mother Dies that her Boy may Live

When the California gold fever broke out, a man went there, leaving his wife in New England with his boy. As soon as he got on and was successful, he was to send for them.

It was a long time before he succeeded, but at last he got money enough to send for them. The wife's heart leaped with joy. She took her boy to New York, got on board a Pacific steamer, and sailed away to San Francisco.

They had not been long at sea before the cry of "Fire! fire!" rang through the ship, and rapidly it gained on them. There was a powder magazine on board, and the captain knew the moment the fire reached the powder, every man, woman, and child would perish.

They got out the lifeboats, but they were too small! In a minute they were overcrowded. The last one was just pushing away, when the mother pleaded with them to take her and her boy. "No," they said, "we have got as many as we can hold."

She entreated them so earnestly that at last they said they would take one more. Do you think she leaped into that boat and left her boy to die? No! She seized her boy, gave him one last hug, kissed him, and dropped him over into the boat.

"My boy," she said, "if you live to see your father, tell him I died in your place."

This is a faint type of what Christ has done for us. He laid down his life for us. He died that we might live. Now, will you not love Him? What would you say of that young man if he should speak contemptuously of such a Savior? May God make us loyal to Christ!

My friends, you will need Him one day. You will need Him when you come to cross the swellings of Jordan. You will need Him when you stand at the bar of God.

Peace

My little boy had some trouble with his sister one Saturday, and he did not want to forgive her. And at night he was going to say his prayers, and I wanted to see how he would say his prayers, and he knelt down by his mother and said his prayers, and then I went up to him, and I said, "Willie, did you pray?"

"I said my prayers."

"Yes, but did you pray?"

"I said my prayers."

"I know you said them, but did you pray?"

He hung his head.

"You are angry with your sister?"

"Well, she had no business to do thus and so."

"That has nothing to do with it; you have the wrong idea, my boy, if you think that you have prayed tonight."

You see, he was trying to get over it by saying, "I said my prayers tonight." I find that people say their prayers every night, just to ease their conscience.

And then I said, "Willie, if you don't forgive your sister, you will not sleep tonight. Ask her to forgive you." He didn't want to do that. He loves the country, and he has been talking a great deal about the time when he can go into the country and play outdoors. So, he said, "Oh, yes, I will sleep well enough; I am going to think about being out there in the country."

That is the way that we are trying to do; we are trying to think of something else to get rid of the thought of these sins, but we cannot. I said nothing more to him. I went on studying, and his mother came down stairs.

But soon he called his mother and said, "Mother, won't you please go up and ask Emma if she won't forgive me?" Then I afterwards heard him murmuring in bed, and he was saying his prayers.

And he said to me, "Papa, you were right, I could not sleep, and I cannot tell you how happy I am now." Don't you think there is any peace until your sins are put away. My dear friends, the gospel of the Lord Jesus Christ is the gospel of peace.

Work Among the Street Arabs

There is an institution in London, in connection with which a gentleman of wealth has done a great deal of good. He went down to the Seven Dials, one of the worst places in London, and there he used to stay till two o'clock in the morning, picking up young street Arabs and taking them into the house of shelter. That man has spent thousands of pounds in that quarter of London.

When I was there he had upwards of three hundred young men, whom he had brought from those slums, who were, some in China, others in Australia, and some in this country. When he would take them from the horrible pit he would have their photographs taken in their rags and dirt. Then they were taken to a bath and given new clothes. They were put into an institution, taught a trade, and not only the rules of life, but every one of them was taught to read his Bible.

After keeping them a few years and educating them, before they left, they were taken to a photograph gallery and had their picture taken, and both were given to them. This was to show them the condition in which the institution found them, and that in which it left them. So, my friends, remember where God found you.

Mrs. Moody Teaching Her Child

There was a time when our little boy did not like to go to church, and would get up in the morning and say to his mother, "What day is tomorrow?"

"Tuesday."

"Next day?"

"Wednesday."

"Next day?"

"Thursday;" and so on, till he came to the answer, "Sunday."
"Dear me," he said.

I said to the mother, "We cannot have our boy grow up to hate Sunday in this way; that will never do. That is the way I used to feel when I was a boy. I used to look upon Sunday with a certain amount of dread. Very few kind words were associated with the day. I don't know that the minister ever put his hand on my head. I don't know that the minister ever noticed me, unless it was when I was asleep in the gallery, and he woke me up. This kind of thing won't do; we must make the Sunday the most attractive day of the week; not a day to be dreaded; but a day of pleasure." Well, the mother took the work up with this boy.

Bless those mothers in their work with the children. Sometimes I feel as if I would rather be the mother of John Wesley, or Martin Luther, or John Knox, than have all the glories in the world. Those mothers who are faithful with the children God has given them will not go unrewarded.

My wife went to work and took those Bible stories and put those blessed truths in a light that the child could comprehend, and soon the feeling of dread for the Sabbath with the boy was the other way. "What day's tomorrow?" he would ask.

"Sunday."

"I am glad."

And if we make those Bible truths interesting – break them up in some shape so that the children can get at them, then they will begin to enjoy them.

Dr. Booth's Story

Dr. Booth of New York, "who has lost all his children" – I say lost, but they are not lost; they are all in heaven – was telling me about being in an eastern country some time ago, and he saw a shepherd going down to a stream, and he wanted to get his flock across.

He went into the water and called them by name, but they came down to the bank and bleated, and were too much afraid to follow. At last he got out of the water, tightened his girdle about his loins, and took up two little lambs and put one inside his frock, and another inside his bosom.

And then he started into the water, and the old ones looked up to the shepherd instead of down into the water. They wanted to see their little ones, and so he got them over the water and led them into the green pastures on the other side.

How many times the Good Shepherd has come down here and taken a little lamb to the hilltops of glory, and then the father and mother begin to look up and follow! Am I not talking to some father or mother that has some loved one gone over the stream? The Good Shepherd has taken it that He may draw you to the world of light, where He has gone to prepare mansions for those that love Him.

Moody Chasing His Shadow

When I was a little boy, I remember I tried to catch my shadow. I don't know if you were ever so foolish; but I remember running after it and trying to get ahead of it. I could not see why the shadow always kept ahead of me.

Once I happened to be racing with my face to the sun, and I looked over my head and saw my shadow coming back of me, and it kept behind me all the way. It is the same with the Son of Righteousness; peace and joy will go with you while you go with your face toward Him, and these people who are getting at the back of the sun are in darkness all the time. Turn to the light of God, and the reflection will flash in your heart. Don't say that God will not forgive you. It is only your will which keeps His forgiveness from you.

A Sad Story

There was an Englishman who had an only son; and only sons are often petted and humored and ruined. This boy became very headstrong, and very often he and his father had trouble.

One day they had a quarrel, and the father was very angry, and so was the son; and the father said he wished the boy would leave home and never come back. The boy said he would go, and would not come into his father's house again till he sent for him. The father said he would never send for him.

Well, away went the boy. But when a father gives up a boy, a mother does not. You mothers will understand that, but the fathers may not. You know there is no love on earth so strong as a mother's love. A great many things may separate a man and his wife; a great many things may separate a father from his son, but there is nothing in the wide world that can ever separate a true mother from her child. To be sure, there are some mothers that have drank so much liquor that they have drunk up all their affection. But I am talking about a true mother; and she would never cast off her boy.

Well, the mother began to write and plead with the boy to write to his father first, and he would forgive him; but the boy said, "I will never go home till father asks me." Then she plead with the father, but the father said, "No, I will never ask him."

At last the mother came down to her sick-bed, broken-hearted, and when she was given up by the physicians to die, the husband, anxious to gratify her last wish, wanted to know if there was nothing he could do for her before she died. The mother gave him a look; he well knew what it meant. Then she said, "Yes, there is one thing you can do. You can send for my boy. That is the only wish on earth you can gratify. If you do not pity him and love him when I am dead and gone, who will?"

"Well," said the father, "I will send word to him that you want to see him."

"No," she says, "you know he will not come for me. If ever I see him you must send for him."

At last the father went to his office and wrote a dispatch in his own name, asking the boy to come home. As soon as he got the invitation from his father, he started off to see his dying mother. When he opened the door to get in, he found his mother dying and his father by the bedside.

The father heard the door open, and saw the boy, but instead of going to meet him, he went to another part of the room, and refused to speak to him. His mother seized his hand; how she had longed to press it! She kissed him, and then said, "Now, my son, just speak to your father. You speak first, and it will all be over."

But the boy said, "No, mother; I will not speak to him until he speaks to me." She took her husband's hand in one hand and the boy's in the other, and spent her dying moments in trying to bring about a reconciliation.

Then, just as she was expiring, she could not speak, so she put the hand of the wayward boy into the hand of the father and passed away. The boy looked at the mother, and the father at the wife, and at last the father's heart broke, and he opened his arms and took that boy to his bosom, and by that body they were reconciled. Sinner, that is only a faint type, a poor illustration, because God is not angry with you.

I bring you tonight to the dead body of Christ. I ask you to look at the wounds in his hands and feet, and the wound in his side. And I ask you, "Will you not be reconciled?"

The Dog Fighter

At one of our meetings in England, a noted dog-fighter was present, and related the following story about himself.

He said he had been carrying on the business of a dog-fighter in the east end of London, and had a very valuable dog, called "Tiger," which had cost a deal of money, and had also won a good deal of money in dog-fights.

Well, he had a fight on the dog for Whit-Monday, for £20; but a few days before that a little child of his died, and it had affected him very much. He did not know what to do to get rid of his feelings, and so he was going to a public-house to have a pipe and something to drink, to help him to forget his sorrow; but as he was going he thought, "Well, there's this Moody and Sankey – suppose I go and hear them?" He went and heard Mr. Moody speak, and came out thinking it was all very good, but did not concern him. His business was very dull, and he had no sport to go to, so he went again.

This time Mr. Aitken was the preacher, and the man said that it appeared as if the preacher left off speaking to the audience and directed his remarks straight at him. He sat down that he should not see him, but he only hit him harder than before.

The service being over, he felt uncomfortable, and went and made inquiries about the matter, and then found that all men were born in sin. After a deal of conversation, and by the grace of God, he was enabled to trust simply in Jesus, and since that time he had been quite happy.

There was his dog; what was he to do with that? Every time he saw Tiger, he saw there was a terrible link between his past life and his present, and he was afraid if he sold the dog, he would only lead someone else into sin. So, he at last decided to destroy the dog, although it cost him a good sum of money and was a very valuable animal. This he did; he tied the dog in a sack and drowned him in the river.

The Prisoner Weeping for His Children

One day in the inquiry room, a man about my age came to me, and he said he wanted to see me alone. I took him one side, and he told me a story that would make almost any man weep.

He was in a good position, a leading business man of the community. He had a beautiful wife and children. He was ambitious to get rich fast, and in an unguarded moment he forged; and in order to cover up that act, he had committed other guilty acts, and he had fled.

He was a fugitive from justice, and he said, "I am now in the torments of hell. Here I am; away from my family. A reward has been offered for me in my city. Do you think I ought to go back?"

I said, "I don't know. You had better go to God and ask Him about it. I would not like to give you advice."

You could hear him sob all over that church. He said, "I

will go to my room, and I will come and see you tomorrow at twelve o'clock."

The next day he came to me, and he said, "I do not belong to myself; I belong to the law. I have got to go and give myself up. I do not care for myself, but it will disgrace my family, but if I don't I am afraid I will lose my soul."

This day I got a letter from him. I think I would like to read it to you. I told some people here of it today, and they said, "You ought to take it to Charlestown, and read it to the convicts in the state prison."

But I thought I had better read it before I got there. It may keep some man from getting there. Someone here may have just commenced. He may tomorrow commit a forgery and bring sorrow and gloom upon his loved ones.

It was only three days ago that I got a letter from a wife and mother, asking me to see her husband. He had committed forgery. The officers came that night and took him. It was a terrible shock to that wife. But let me read the letter.

Jefferson City, Mo., April 8, 1877.

Mr. Moody:

Dear Brother: When I bade you good-bye in Farwell hall, you said, "When it is all over, write me." I wrote you in December. I thought then that it would soon be over. [Let me say right here that that letter which came in December drew a picture that has followed me all these days. He said he went to his home.

The trial was to come off in another county. He wanted to see his wife, and he went to his home. He did not want his children to know that he was at home, because it might get out among the neighbors, and he wanted to give himself up and not be arrested.

Then after his wife had put the children to bed, he would steal into the room, but he could not speak to them or kiss them. Fathers, was not that pretty hard? Would not that be pretty hard? You tell me sin is sweet! There are men with their eyes wide open; no, not with their eyes wide open; they must be closed when men say that sin is sweet. There is that man that loved his children as you love yours, and he did not dare to speak to them.]

I wrote you in December, thinking all would soon be over, but the state was not ready to try me, and so I was let out upon bail till April. Yesterday my case was disposed of, and I received sentence for nineteen years. [Oh, how sad; how bitter sin is! May God open the eyes of the blind! Christians, always pray that God may open the eyes of the blind. Christ came for the recovery of sight to the blind. I hope every sinner will get his eyes open and see that sin is bitter and not sweet. The time is coming when you have got to leave this earth.]

Now I am in my prison cell, clothed in a convict's garb. It is all over with me. A long term of civil death and absence. [Then there is a long dash. I suppose he could not pen it. Away from that wife and those dear children!]

Now I have met the law. Pray for me that I may be sustained with consoling and needed strength. Pray for the loved ones at home; my dear parents, and brothers and sisters, and my dear wife and children. [Another long dash.] And I ask that the attorney that was very kind to me may be prayed for, that he may become a Christian. And if not asking too much, a few words will be gratefully received.

Address me in care of penitentiary in Jefferson City, Mo. I pray that your labors may be blessed, and when you preach, warn men to beware of the temptation of doing evil that good may come of it; warn them to beware of the ambition for wealth.

Prayerfully and tearfully yours.

The Forger's Children

The Child and President Lincoln

During the war I remember a young man not twenty, who was court-martialed down in the front and sentenced to be shot. The story was this:

The young fellow had enlisted. He was not obliged to, but he went off with another young man. They were what we would call "chums." One night this companion was ordered out on picket duty, and he asked the young man to go for him.

The next night he was ordered out himself, and having been awake two nights and not being used to it, fell asleep at his post, and for the offense he was tried and sentenced to death. It was right after the order issued by the president that no interference would be allowed in cases of this kind. This sort of thing had become too frequent, and it must be stopped.

When the news reached the father and mother in Vermont, it nearly broke their hearts. The thought that their son should be shot was too great for them. They had no hope that he would be saved by anything they could do.

But they had a little daughter who had read the life of Abraham Lincoln, and knew how he had loved his own children, and she said, "If Abraham Lincoln knew how my father and mother loved my brother, he wouldn't let him be shot."

That little girl thought the matter over and made up her mind to see the president. She went to the White House, and the sentinel, when he saw her imploring looks, passed her in, and when she came to the door and told the private secretary that she wanted to see the president, he could not refuse her.

She came into the chamber and found Abraham Lincoln surrounded by his generals and counselors, and when he saw the little country girl, he asked her what she wanted.

The little maid told her plain, simple story; how her brother, whom her father and mother loved very dearly, had been sentenced to be shot; how they were mourning for him, and if he was to die in that way it would break their hearts.

The president's heart was touched with compassion, and he immediately sent a dispatch canceling the sentence, and giving the boy a parole so that he could come home and see that father and mother.

I just tell you this to show you how Abraham Lincoln's heart was moved by compassion for the sorrow of that father and mother, and if he showed so much, do you think the Son of God will not have compassion upon you, sinner, if you only take that crushed, bruised heart to Him?

Moody in the Far West

I remember when I went to California just to try and get a few souls saved on the Pacific coast. I went into a school there, and asked, "Have you got someone who can write a plain hand?"

"Yes."

Well, we got up the blackboard, and the lesson upon it

proved to be the very text we have tonight. "Lay up for yourselves treasures in heaven."

And I said, "Suppose we write upon that board some of the earthly treasures? And we will begin with 'gold.'"

The teacher readily put down "gold," and they all comprehended it, for all had run to that country in hope of finding it.

"Well, we will put down 'houses' next, and then 'land.' Next we will put down 'fast horses.'" They all understood what fast horses were; they knew a good deal more about fast horses than they knew about the kingdom of God. Some of them, I think, actually made fast horses serve as gods.

"Next we will put down 'tobacco.'" The teacher seemed to shrink at this. "Put it down," said I; "many a man thinks more of tobacco than he does of God.

Well, then we will put down 'rum.'" He objected to this; didn't like to put it down at all. "Down with it! Many a man will sell his reputation, will sell his home, his wife, his children, everything he has, for rum. It is the god of some men. Many here are ready to sell their present and their eternal welfare for it. Put it down;" and down it went.

"Now," said I, "suppose we put down some of the heavenly treasures. Put down 'Jesus' to head the list, then 'heaven,' then 'river of life,' then 'crown of glory,'" and we went on until the column was filled, and then just drew a line and showed the heavenly and the earthly things in contrast. My friends, they could not stand comparison. If a man just does that, he cannot but see the superiority of the heavenly over the earthly treasures.

Well, it turned out that the teacher was not a Christian. He had gone to California on the usual hunt – gold; and when he saw the two columns placed side by side, the excellence of the one over the other was irresistible, and he was the first soul God gave me on the Pacific coast. He accepted Christ, and that man came to the station when I was coming away and blessed me for coming to that place.

The Little Orphan

When I was in Europe, Mr. Spurgeon told me a story of a boy who was in an orphan asylum. This little boy came up to Mr. Spurgeon and said, "Mr. Spurgeon, would you allow me to speak to you?"

He said, "Certainly; get upon my knee."

The little fellow got up and said, "Mr. Spurgeon, supposing that your mother was dead, and that your father was dead; and that you were put into this institution; and that there were other little boys that had no father or mother, but that they had cousins and uncles and aunts, and that they brought them fruit and candy and a lot of things. Don't you think that you would feel bad? 'Cause that's me."

Why, Mr. Spurgeon put his hand in his pocket, and gave the little fellow some money right off. The little fellow had pleaded his cause well.

When men come to God and tell their story – I don't care how vile you are; I don't care how far down you have got; I don't care how far off you have wandered – if you will tell it all into His ear, the relief will soon come.

Moody's Mother and Her Prodigal Son

I can give you a little experience of my own family. Before I was fourteen years old, the first thing I remember was the death of my father. He had been unfortunate in business and failed. Soon after his death the creditors came in and took everything. My mother was left with a large family of children.

One calamity after another swept over the entire household. Twins were added to the family, and my mother was taken sick. The eldest boy was fifteen years of age, and to him my mother looked as a stay in her calamity, but all at once that boy became a wanderer. He had been reading some of the trashy novels, and the belief had seized him that he had only to go away to make a fortune.

Away he went. I can remember how eagerly she used to look for tidings of that boy, how she used to send to the post-office to see if there was a letter from him, and recollect how we used to come back with the sad tidings, "No letter."

I remember how in the evenings we used to sit beside her in that New England home, and we would talk about our father, but the moment the name of that boy was mentioned she would hush us into silence.

Some nights when the wind was very high, and the house, which was upon a hill, would tremble at every gust, the voice of my mother was raised in prayer for that wanderer who had treated her so unkindly. I used to think she loved him more than all the rest of us put together, and I believe she did. On a Thanksgiving day – you know that is a family day in New England – she used to set a chair for him, thinking he would return home.

Her family grew up, and her boys left home. When I got so that I could write, I sent letters all over the country, but could find no trace of him.

One day while in Boston, the news reached me that he had returned. While in that city, I remember how I used to look for him in every store – he had a mark on his face – but I never got any trace.

One day while my mother was sitting at the door, a stranger was seen coming toward the house, and when he came to the door he stopped. My mother didn't know her boy. He stood there with folded arms, and great beard flowing down his breast, his tears trickling down his face. When my mother saw those tears she cried, "Oh, it is my lost son," and entreated him to come in.

But he stood still. "No, mother," he said, "I will not come in, till I hear first you have forgiven me." Do you believe she was not willing to forgive him? Do you think she was likely to keep him long standing there? She rushed to the threshold, and threw her arms around him, and breathed forgiveness. God will forgive you.

Jump into Father's Arms

I remember, while in Mobile attending meetings, a little incident occurred which I will relate. It was a beautiful evening, and just before the meeting some neighbors and myself were sitting on the front piazza enjoying the evening. One of the neighbors put one of his children upon a ledge eight feet high, and put out his hands and told him to jump.

Without the slightest hesitation, he sprang into his father's arms. Another child was lifted up, and he, too, readily sprang into the arms of his father. He picked up another boy, larger than the others, and held out his arms, but he wouldn't jump.

He cried and screamed to be taken down. The man begged the boy to jump, but it was of no use; he couldn't be induced to jump. The incident made me curious, and I stepped up to him and asked, "How was it that those two little fellows jumped so readily into your arms, and the other boy wouldn't?"

"Why," said the man, "those two boys are my children, and the other boy isn't; he don't know me."

A Child Legend

There is a beautiful legend told about a little girl who was the first-born of a family in Egypt, when the destroying angel swept through that land, and consequently who would have been a victim on that night if the protecting blood were not sprinkled on the door posts of her father's house.

The order was that the first born should be struck by death all through Egypt. This little girl was sick, and she knew that death would take her, and she might be a victim of the order. She asked her father if the blood was sprinkled on the doorposts. He said it was, that he had ordered it to be done. She asked him if he had seen it there. He said no, but he had no doubt that it was done. He had seen the lamb killed and had told the servant to attend to it.

But she was not satisfied and asked her father to go and see and urged him to take her in his arms and carry her to the door to see. They found that the servant had neglected to put the blood upon the posts. There the child was exposed to death until they found the blood and sprinkled it on the posts, and then it was safe. Personally see to it that you are safe in Christ.

Sammy and His Mother

At one time my sister had trouble with her little boy, and the father said, "Why, Sammy, you must go now and ask your mother's forgiveness." The little fellow said he wouldn't.

The father says, "You must. If you don't go and ask your mother's forgiveness, I shall have to undress you and put you to bed."

He was a bright, nervous little fellow, never still a moment, and the father thought he would have such a dread of being undressed and put to bed. But the little fellow wouldn't, so they undressed him and put him to bed.

The father went to his business, and when he came home at noon he said to his wife, "Has Sammy asked your forgiveness?"

"No," she said; "he hasn't."

So, the father went to him, and said, "Why, Sammy, why don't you ask your mother's forgiveness?"

The little fellow shook his head, "Won't do it."

"But, Sammy, you have got to."

"Couldn't."

The father went down to his office, and stayed all the afternoon, and when he came home he asked his wife, "Has Sammy asked your forgiveness?"

"No; I took something up to him and tried to have him eat, but he wouldn't."

So, the father went up to see him, and said, "Now, Sammy,

just ask your mother's forgiveness, and you may be dressed and come down to supper with us."

"Couldn't do it."

The father coaxed, but the little fellow "couldn't do it."

That was all they could get out of him. You know very well he could, but he didn't want to. Now, the hardest thing a man has to do is to become a Christian, and it is the easiest. That may seem a contradiction, but it isn't. The hard point is because he doesn't want to. The hardest thing for a man to do is to give up his will.

That night they retired, and they thought surely, early in the morning, he will be ready to ask his mother's forgiveness. The father went to him – that was Friday morning – to see if he was ready to ask his mother's forgiveness, but he "couldn't."

The father and mother felt so bad about it they couldn't eat; they thought it was to darken their whole life. Perhaps that boy thought that father and mother didn't love him. Just what many sinners think because God won't let them have their own way.

The father went to his business, and when he came home he said to his wife, "Has Sammy asked your forgiveness?"

"No." So he went to the little fellow, and said, "Now, Sammy, are you not going to ask your mother's forgiveness?"

"Can't," and that was all they could get out of him.

The father couldn't eat any dinner; it was like death in the house. It seemed as if the boy was going to conquer his father and mother. Instead of his little will being broken, it looked very much as if he was going to break theirs.

Late Friday afternoon, "Mother, mother, forgive," says Sammy, "me." And the little fellow said "me," and he sprang to his feet, and said, "I have said it, I have said it. Now, dress me, and take me down to see father. He will be so glad to know I have said it." And she took him down, and when the little fellow came in, he said, "I've said it, I've said it."

Oh, my friends, it is so easy to say, "I will arise and go to my God." It is the most reasonable thing you can do. Isn't it an unreasonable thing to hold out? Come right to God just this very hour. "Believe on the Lord Jesus Christ, and thou shalt be saved."

A Singular Story

When I was a young boy – before I was a Christian – I was in a field one day with a man who was hoeing. He was weeping, and he told me a strange story, which I have never forgotten.

When he left home his mother gave him this text, "Seek first the kingdom of God." But he paid no heed to it. He said when he got settled in life, and his ambition to get money was gratified, it would be time enough then to seek the kingdom of God.

He went from one village to another and got nothing to do. When Sunday came, he went into a village church, and what was his great surprise to hear the minister give out the text, "Seek first the kingdom of God."

He said the text went down to the bottom of his heart. He thought that it was but his mother's prayer following him, and that someone must have written to that minister about him. He felt very uncomfortable, and when the meeting was over he could not get that sermon out of his mind.

He went away from that town, and at the end of a week went

into another church, and he heard the minister give out the same text, "Seek first the kingdom of God." He felt sure this time that it was the prayers of his mother, but he said calmly and deliberately, "No; I will first get wealthy."

He said he went on and did not go into a church for a few months, but the first place of worship he went into, he heard a third minister preaching a sermon from the same text. He tried to drown, to stifle his feelings; tried to get the sermon out of his mind and resolved that he would keep away from church altogether, and for a few years did keep out of God's house.

"My mother died," he said, "and the text kept coming up in my mind, and I said I will try and become a Christian." The tears rolled down his cheeks as he said, "I could not; no sermon ever touches me; my heart is as hard as that stone," pointing to one in the field. I couldn't understand what it was all about; it was fresh to me then. I went to Boston and got converted, and the first thought that came to me was about this man. When I got back, I asked my mother, "Is Mr. L_____ living in such a place?"

"Didn't I write to you about him?" she asked. "They have taken him to an insane asylum, and to everyone who goes there, he points with his finger up there, and tells him to 'seek first the kingdom of God.'" There was that man with his eyes dull with the loss of reason, but the text had sunk into his soul; it had burned down deep. Oh, may the Spirit of God burn the text into your hearts tonight!

When I got home again my mother told me he was in her house, and I went to see him. I found him in a rocking chair, with that vacant, idiotic look upon him. Whenever he saw me he pointed at me, and said, "Young man, seek first the kingdom of God."

Reason was gone, but the text was there. Last month when I was laying my brother down in his grave, I could not help thinking of that poor man who was lying so near him, and wishing that the prayer of his mother had been heard and that he had found the kingdom of God.

Humility

I suppose Isaiah thought he was as good as most men in his day, and perhaps he was a good deal better than most men, but when he saw the Lord, he cried, "Woe is me, for I am undone; because I am a man of unclean lips."

When he saw the Lord, he saw his own deformity, and he fell in the dust before the Lord. And that is the proper place for a sinner. As I have said before, until men realize their uncleanness, they talk of their own righteousness, but the moment they catch a sight of Him their mouth is stopped.

If we hear a man talking about himself, we may be sure that he has not seen God. Look at that man Daniel. Not a thing can be found against him, but see when he came within sight of God. He found that his comeliness turned to corruption.

And look at Job. One would have thought that he was all right. He was good to the poor, liberal to all charities; not a better man within a thousand miles. If they wanted to get a thousand dollars to endow a university, a thousand dollars to build a synagogue, if they wanted a thousand dollars for any charitable object, why, he was the man. Why, you would have liked to get him into your Presbyterian, or Methodist, or Baptist churches; if you wanted a chairman of a benevolent society, you couldn't have found a better man.

Yet look at him when God came near him. It is altogether different when He comes within our sight. It is one thing to hear Him, and another thing to see Him. He had heard Him with his ears, but now he saw Him with his eyes, and then he was silent. You couldn't get another word from him. Before he saw Him, he could argue and talk about Him to his friends, could argue as well as they could; but the moment Job saw Him he was silent.

When He said, "Gird up thy loins like a man," from that time he put no more questions to Him. He had got a lesson. No man can come into His kingdom till he knows he is vile, till he sees Him. He must come down to that. That is God's alphabet.

The Child and the Infidel

I remember hearing of a Sabbath school teacher who had led every one of her children to Christ. She was a faithful teacher. Then she tried to get her children to go out and bring other children into the school.

One day one of them came and said she had been trying to get the children of a family to come to the school, but the father was an infidel and he wouldn't allow it. "What is an infidel?" asked the child. She had never heard of an infidel before.

The teacher went on to tell her what an infidel man was,

and she was perfectly shocked. A few mornings after, the girl happened to be going past the post office on her way to school, and she saw the infidel father coming out. She went up to him, and said, "Why don't you love Jesus?"

If it had been a man who had said that to him, probably he would have knocked him down. He looked at her and walked on.

A second time she put the question, "Why don't you love Jesus?" He put out his hand to put her gently away from him, when, on looking down, he saw her in tears. "Please, sir, tell me why you don't love Jesus."

He pushed her aside and away he went. When he got to his office, he couldn't get this question out of his mind. All the letters seemed to read, "Why don't you love Jesus?" All men in his place of business seemed to say, "Why don't you love Jesus?"

When he tried to write, his pen seemed to shape the words, "Why don't you love Jesus?" He couldn't rest, and on the street he went to mingle with the business men, but he seemed to hear a voice continually asking him, "Why don't you love Jesus?" He thought when night came and he got home with his family, he would forget it; but he couldn't. He complained that he wasn't well and went to bed. But when he laid his head on the pillow, that voice kept whispering, "Why don't you love Jesus?"

He couldn't sleep. By-and-by, about midnight, he got up, and said, "I will get a Bible, and find where Christ contradicts Himself, and then I'll have a reason," and he turned to the book of John. My friends, if you want a reason for not loving Christ, don't turn to John. He knew Him too long. I don't believe a man can read the gospel of John without being turned to Christ.

Well, he read through, and found no reason why he shouldn't love Him, but he found many reasons why he should. He read this book, and before morning he was on his knees, and that question put by that little child led to his conversion.

Picking up the Bible

The hardest thing, I will admit, ever a man had to do is to become a Christian, and yet it is the easiest. This seems to many to be a paradox, but I will repeat it; it is the most difficult thing to become a Christian, and yet it is the easiest.

I have a little nephew in Chicago. When he was three or four years of age, he threw that Bible on the floor. I think a good deal of that Bible, and I didn't like to see this. His mother said to him, "Go, pick up your uncle's Bible from the floor."

"I won't," he replied.

"Go and pick that Bible up directly."

"I won't."

"What did you say?" asked his mother. She thought he didn't understand.

But he understood well enough, and had made up his mind that he wouldn't. She told the boy she would have to punish him if he didn't, and then he said he couldn't, and by-and-by he said he didn't want to.

And that is the way with the people in coming to Christ. At first, they say they won't, then they can't, and then they don't want to. The mother insisted upon the boy picking up the Bible, and he got down and put his arms around it and pretended he couldn't lift it. He was a great, healthy boy, and he could have picked it up easily enough.

I was very anxious to see the fight carried on, because she was a young mother, and if she didn't break that boy's will, he was going to break her heart by-and- by. So she told him again, if he didn't pick it up, she would punish him, and the child just picked it up. It was very easy to do it when he made up his mind. So, it is perfectly easy for men to accept the gospel. The trouble is, they don't want to give up their will.

If you want to be saved, you must just accept that gospel; that Christ is your Savior; that He is your redeemer, and that He has rescued you from the curse of the law. Just say, "Lord Jesus Christ, I trust you from this hour to save me"; and the moment you take that stand, He will put His loving arms around you and wrap about you the robe of righteousness.

Johnny Cling Close to the Rock

Little Johnny and his sister were one day going through a long, narrow tunnel. The railroad company had built small clefts here and there through the tunnel, so that if any one got caught in the tunnel when the train was passing, they could save themselves.

After this little boy and girl had gone some distance in the tunnel, they heard a train coming. They were frightened at first, but the sister just put her little brother in one cleft, and she hurried and hid in another. The train came thundering along, and as it passed, the sister cried out, "Johnny, cling close to the rock! Johnny, cling close to the rock!" and they were safe.

The "Rock of Ages" may be beaten by the storms and waves

of adversity, but "cling close to the rock," Christians, and all will be well. The waves don't touch the Christian; he is sheltered by the Rock "that is higher than I," by the One who is the strong arm, and the Savior who is mighty and willing to save.

The Saloon Keeper and his Children

I remember when I first began to work for the Lord, fifteen or sixteen years ago, there was a Boston business man who was converted there and stayed three months, and when leaving he said to me that there was a man living on such a street in whom he was very much interested, and whose boy was in the high school, and he had said that he had two brothers and a little sister who didn't go anywhere to Sabbath school, because their parents would not let them.

This gentleman said, "I wish you would go round and see them." Well, I went, and I found that the parents lived in a drinking saloon, and that the father kept the bar. I stepped up to him and told him what I wanted, and he said he would rather have his sons become drunkards, and his daughter a harlot, than have them go to our schools.

I thought that it looked pretty dark, and that he was pretty bitter to me, but I went a second time, thinking that I might catch him in a better humor. He ordered me out again.

I went a third time and found him in better humor. He said,

"You are talking too much about the Bible. Well, I will tell you what I will do; if you teach them something reasonable, like 'Paine's Age of Reason,' they may go." Then I talked further to him, and finally he said, "If you will read Paine's book, I will read the New Testament."

Well, to get hold of him I promised, and he got the best of the bargain. We exchanged books, and that gave me a chance to call again and talk with that family. One day he said, "Young man, you have talked so much about church, now you can have a church down here."

"What do you mean?"

"Why, I will invite some friends, and you can come down here and preach to them; not that I believe a word you say, but I do it to see if it will do us chaps any good."

"Very well," I said; "now let us have it distinctly understood that we are to have a certain definite time."

He told me to come at 11 o'clock, saying, "I want you to understand that you are not to do all the preaching."

"How is that?"

"I shall want to talk some, and also my friends."

I said, "Supposing we have it understood that you are to have forty minutes and I fifteen, is that fair?"

Well, he thought it was *fair*. He was to have the first forty and I the last fifteen minutes. I went down, and, behold, the saloon-keeper wasn't there. I thought perhaps he had backed out, but I found that the reason was that he had found that his saloon was not large enough to hold all his friends, and he had gone to a neighbor's, whither I went and found two rooms filled.

There were atheists, infidels, and scoffers there. I had taken a little boy with me, thinking he might aid me. The moment I got in, they plied me with all sorts of questions, but I said I hadn't come to hold any discussion; that they had been discussing for years and had reached no conclusion.

They took up the forty-five minutes of time talking, and the result was there was no two who could agree. Then came my turn. I said, "We always open our meetings with prayer; let us pray." I prayed and thought perhaps someone else would pray before I got through.

After I finished the little boy prayed. I wish you could have heard him. He prayed to God to have mercy upon those men who were talking so against His beloved Son. His voice sounded more like an angel's than a human voice. After we got up, I was going to speak, but there was not a dry eye in the assembly.

One after another went out, and the old man I had been after for months, and sometimes it had looked pretty dark, came, and putting his hands on my shoulder, with tears streaming down his face, said, "Mr. Moody, you can have my children go to your Sunday school."

The next Sunday they came, and after a few months the oldest boy, a promising young man then in the high school, came upon the platform, and with his chin quivering and the tears in his eyes, said, "I wish to ask these people to pray for me; I want to become a Christian." God heard and answered our prayers for him.

In all my acquaintances, I don't know of a man whom it seemed more hopeless to reach. I believe if we lay ourselves out for the work, there is not a man in this city but can be reached and saved. I don't care who he is; if we go in the name of our Master, and persevere until we succeed, it will not be long before Christ will bless us, no matter how hard their heart is.

"We shall reap if we faint not." I didn't have a warmer friend in Chicago; he was true to me.

Love in a Sunday School

John Wanamaker, superintendent of probably one of the largest Sunday schools in the world, had a theory that he would never put a boy out of his school for bad conduct. He argued if a boy misbehaved himself, it was through bad training at home, and that if he put him out of the school, no one would take care of him.

Well, this theory was put to the test one day. A teacher came to him, and said, "I've got a boy in my class that must be taken out; he breaks the rules continually, he swears and uses obscene language, and I cannot do anything with him."

Mr. Wanamaker did not care about putting the boy out, so he sent the teacher back to his class. But he came again and said that unless the boy was taken from his class, he must leave it.

Well, he left, and a second teacher was appointed. The second teacher came with the same story and met with the same reply from Mr. Wanamaker. And he resigned.

A third teacher was appointed, and he came with the same story as the others. Mr. Wanamaker then thought he would be compelled to turn the boy out at last.

One day a few teachers were standing about, and Mr. Wanamaker said, "I will bring this boy up and read his name out in the school, and publicly excommunicate him." Well, a young lady came up and said to him, "I am not doing what I might for Christ; let me have the boy; I will try and save him." But Mr. Wanamaker said, "If these young men cannot do it, you will not." But she begged to have him, and Mr. Wanamaker consented.

She was a wealthy young lady, surrounded with all the luxuries of life. The boy went to her class, and for several Sundays he behaved himself and broke no rule. But one Sunday he broke one, and, in reply to something she said, spit in her face. She took out her pocket handkerchief and wiped her face, but she said nothing.

Well, she thought upon a plan, and she said to him, "John" – we will call him John – "John, come home with me."

"No," says he; "I won't; I won't be seen on the streets with you."

She was fearful of losing him altogether if he went out of the school that day, and she said, "Will you let me walk home with you?"

"No, I won't," said he; "I won't be seen on the street with you."

Then she thought upon another plan. She thought on the "Old Curiosity Shop," and she said, "I won't be at home tomorrow or Tuesday, but if you will come round to the front door on Wednesday morning there will be a little bundle for you."

"I don't want it; you may keep your own bundle."

She went home, but made the bundle up. She thought that curiosity might make him come.

Wednesday morning arrived, and he had got over his mad fit and thought he would just like to see what was in that bundle. The little fellow knocked at the door, which was opened, and he told his story. She said, "Yes, here is the bundle." The boy opened it and found a vest, and a coat and other clothing, and a little note written by the young lady, which read something like this:

> "Dear Johnnie: Ever since you have been in my class I have prayed for you every morning and evening, that you might be a good boy, and I want you to come to my class. Do not leave me."

The next morning, before she was up, the servant came to her and said there was a little boy below who wished to see her. She dressed hastily, and went down stairs, and found Johnnie on the sofa weeping. She put her arms around his neck, and he said to her, "My dear teacher, I have not had any peace since I got this note from you. I want you to forgive me."

"Won't you let me pray for you to come to Jesus?" replied the teacher; and she went down on her knees and prayed. And now Mr. Wanamaker says that boy is the best boy in his Sunday school. And so it was love that won that boy's heart.

The Loved One and the Lover

There are a great many things to separate a man from his wife, or one friend from another; but the mother's love is generally unchangeable. Her son may be a murderer; public opinion may be against him; the daily journals may write him down; his friends may forsake him, but that mother will take her stand in the court beside her boy. The jury may give a verdict against him, and he may be sentenced to death; but you will find that mother going down to his cell, and she will love him through it all.

She doesn't care for public opinion; she don't heed the sentiments of the press. Everything may be gone from her, but love for her son will remain. And when that son has been executed, and life has left his body, she will go down to his grave and water it with tears, and will cherish the memory of that boy as long as she lives. But all this is not to be compared with the love of God. God's love is not confined to one man; it is universal and unfailing and unchangeable.

The Cross

While down at a convention in Illinois, an old man past seventy years said he remembered but one thing about his father, and that one thing followed him all through life. He could not remember his death, he had no recollection of his funeral, but he recollected his father, one winter night, taking a little chip, and with his pocket knife whittling out a little cross, and told how God in His infinite love sent His Son down here to redeem us; how He had died on the cross for us. The story of the cross followed him through life; and I tell you if you teach these children truths, they will follow them through life.

For Charlie's Sake

In Detroit, at an international convention of the Young Men's Christian Association, Judge Olds was present as a delegate from Columbus. One evening he was telling about the mighty power Christians summon to their aid in the petition "for Christ's sake," "in Jesus' name," and he told a story that made a great impression on me. When the war came on, he said, his only son left for the army, and he became suddenly interested in soldiers.

Every soldier that passed by brought his son to remembrance; he could see his son in him. He went to work for soldiers. When a sick soldier came there to Columbus one day, so weak he couldn't walk, the judge took him in a carriage, and got him into the soldier's home. Soon he became president of the soldier's home in Columbus, and used to go down every day and spend hours in looking after those soldiers and seeing that they had every comfort.

He spent on them a great deal of time and a great deal of money. One day he said to his wife, "I'm giving too much time to these soldiers. I've got to stop it. There's an important case coming on in court, and I've got to attend to my own business."

He said he went down to the office that morning, resolved in future to let the soldiers alone. He went to his desk, and then to writing. Pretty soon the door opened, and he saw a soldier hobble slowly in. He started at sight of him. The man was fumbling at something in his breast, and pretty soon he got out an old soiled paper. The father saw it was his own son's writing.

"Dear Father: This young man belongs to my company. He has lost his leg and his health in defense of his country, and he is going home to his mother to die. If he calls on you, treat him kindly.

"For Charlie's Sake."

"For Charlie's sake." The moment he saw that, a pang went to his heart. He got up for a carriage, lifted the maimed soldier, drove home, put him into Charlie's room, sent for the family physician, kept him in the family, and treated him like his own son.

When the young soldier got well enough to go to the train to go home to his mother, he took him to the railway station, put him in the nicest, most comfortable place in the carriage, and sent him on his way home to his mother. "I did it," said the old judge, "for Charlie's sake." Now, whatsoever you do, my friends, do it for the Lord Jesus' sake. Do and ask everything in His name, in the name of Him "who loved us and gave Himself for us."

The Orange Boy

One day as a young lady was walking up the street, she saw a little boy running out of a shoemaker's shop, and behind him was the old shoemaker chasing him with a wooden last in his hand. He had not run far until the last was thrown at him, and he was struck in the back.

The boy stopped and began to cry. The Spirit of the Lord touched that young lady's heart, and she went to where he was. She stepped up to him and asked him if he was hurt. He told her it was none of her business. She went to work then to win that boy's confidence.

She asked him if he went to school. He said, "No."

"Well, why don't you go to school?"

"Don't want to."

She asked him if he would not like to go to Sunday school. "If you will come," she said, "I will tell you beautiful stories and read nice books." She coaxed and pleaded with him, and at last said that if he would consent to go, she would meet him on the corner of a street which they should agree upon.

He at last consented, and the next Sunday, true to his promise, he waited for her at the place designated. She took him by the hand and led him into the Sabbath school. "Can you give me a place to teach this little boy?" she asked of the superintendent.

He looked at the boy, but they didn't have any such looking little ones in the school. A place was found, however, and she sat down in the corner and tried to win that soul for Christ.

Many would look upon that with contempt, but she had got something to do for the Master. The little boy had never heard anybody sing so sweetly before.

When he went home he was asked where he had been. "Been among the angels," he told his mother. He said he had been to the Protestant Sabbath school, but his father and mother told him he must not go there any more, or he would get a flogging.

The next Sunday he went, and when he came home, he got the promised flogging. He went the second time and got a flogging, and also a third time with the same result. At last he said to his father, "I wish you would flog me before I go, and then I won't have to think of it when I am there."

The father said, "If you go to that Sabbath school again, I will kill you." It was the father's custom to send his son out on the street to sell articles to the passers-by, and he told the boy that he might have the profits of what he sold on Saturday.

The little fellow hastened to the young lady's house, and said to her, "Father said that he would give me every Saturday to myself, and if you will just teach me, then I will come to your house every Saturday afternoon." I wonder how many young ladies there are that would give up their Saturday afternoons just to lead one boy into the kingdom of God.

Every Saturday afternoon that little boy was there at her house, and she tried to tell him the way to Christ. She labored with him, and at last the light of God's spirit broke upon his heart.

One day, while he was selling his wares at the railroad station, a train of cars approached unnoticed, and passed over both his legs. A physician was summoned, and the first thing after he arrived the little sufferer looked up into his face, and said, "Doctor, will I live to get home?"

"No," said the doctor; "you are dying."

"Will you tell my mother and father that I died a Christian?"

They bore home the boy's corpse, and with it the last

message that he died a Christian. Oh, what a noble work was that young lady's in saving that little wanderer! How precious the remembrance to her! When she goes to heaven, she will not be a stranger there. He will take her by the hand and lead her to the throne of Christ. She did the work cheerfully. Oh, may God teach us what our work is, that we may do it for His glory!

The Orange Boy

Finding Your Picture

You know I have an idea that the Bible is like an album. I go into a man's house, and while waiting for him, I take up an album and open it. I look at a picture. "Why, that looks like a man I know." I turn over and look at another. "Well, I know that man." By-and-by I come upon another. "Why, that man looks like my brother." I am getting pretty near home. I keep turning over the leaves. "Well, I declare, there is a man who lives in the street I do; why, he is my next-door neighbor." And then I come upon another, and I see myself.

My friends, if you read your Bibles, you will find your own pictures there. It will just describe you. Now, it may be there is some Pharisee here tonight; if there is, let him turn to the third chapter of John, and see what Christ said to that Pharisee. "Except a man be born again, he cannot enter the kingdom of God." Nicodemus, no doubt, was one of the fairest specimens of a man in Jerusalem in those days, yet he had to be born again, else he couldn't see the kingdom of God.

But you may say, "I am not a Pharisee; I am a poor, miserable sinner, too bad to come to Him." Well, turn to the woman of Samaria and see what He said to her. See what a difference there was between that publican and that Pharisee. There was as great a distance between them as between the sun and the moon. One was in the very highest station, and the other occupied the very worst. One had only himself and his sins to bring to God, the other was trying to bring in his position and his aristocracy. I tell you, when a man gets a true sight of himself, all his position and station and excellences drop.

See this prayer, "'I thank God,' 'I am not,' 'I fast,' 'I give,' 'I possess.'" Why, if he had delivered a long prayer and it had been put into the hands of printers, they would have to send out for some 'I's. "I thank God." "I, I, I."

When a man prays, not with himself, but to God, he does not exalt himself; he doesn't pass a eulogy upon himself. He falls flat down in dust before God. In that prayer you don't find him thanking God for what He had done for him. It was a heathen, prayerless prayer, merely a form.

I hope the day will come when formal prayers will be a thing of the past. I think the reason why we cannot get more people out to the meetings is because we have too many formal prayers in the churches. These formal Christians get up like this Pharisee and thank God they are not like other men; but when a man gets a look at himself, he prays with the spirit of the publican.

A Bad Boy

I once heard of a father who had a prodigal boy, and the boy had sent his mother down to the grave with a broken heart. One evening the boy started out as usual to spend the night in drinking and gambling, and his old father, as he was leaving, said, "My son, I want to ask a favor of you tonight. You have not spent an evening with me since your mother died. Now, won't you gratify your old father by staying at home with him?"

"No," said the young man, "it is lonely here, and there is nothing to interest me, and I am going out."

And the old man prayed and wept, and at last said, "My boy, you are just killing me as you have killed your mother. These hairs are growing white, and you are sending me, too, to the grave."

Still the boy would not stay, and the old man said, "If you are determined to go to ruin, you must go over this old body tonight. I cannot resist you. You are stronger than I, but if you go out, you must go over this body." And he laid himself down before the door, and that son walked over the form of his father, trampled the love of his father under foot, and went out.

Saved in Weakness

Doctor Andrew Bonar told me how, in the highlands of Scotland, often sheep would wander off into the rocks and get into places that they couldn't get out of. The grass on these mountains is very sweet, and the sheep like it, and they will jump down ten or twelve feet, and then they can't jump back again, and the shepherd hears them bleating in distress. They may be there for days until they have eaten all the grass, and he will wait until they are so faint they cannot stand, and then they put a rope around him and he will go over there and pull that sheep up out of the jaws of death.

"Why don't they go down there when the sheep first gets there?" I asked.

"Ah!" he said, "they are so very foolish they would dash right over the precipice and be killed if they did!"

And that is the way with men; they won't go back to God till they have no friends and have lost everything. If you are a wanderer, I come to tell you that the Good Shepherd will bring you back the moment you have given up trying to save yourself and are willing to let Him save you His own way.

Young Moody at School

I remember, when a boy, I used to go to a certain school in New England, where we had a quick-tempered master, who always kept a rattan. It was, "If you don't do this, and don't do that, I'll punish you." I remember many a time of this rattan being laid upon my back. I think I can almost feel it now.

He used to rule that school by the law. But after a while there was somebody who began to get up a movement in favor of controlling the school by love. A great many said, "You can never do that with those unruly boys," but after some talk it was at last decided to try it.

I remember how we thought of the good time we would have that winter when the rattan would be out of the school.

We thought we would then have all the fun we wanted. I remember who the teacher was; it was a lady, and she opened the school with prayer. We hadn't seen it done before, and we were impressed, especially when she prayed that she might have grace and strength to rule the school with love.

Well, the school went on for several weeks, and we saw no rattan, but at last the rules were broken, and I think I was the first boy to break them. She told me to wait till after school, and then she would see me.

I thought the rattan was coming out sure and stretched myself up in war-like attitude. After school, however, I didn't see the rattan, but she sat down by me and told me how she loved me, and how she had prayed to be able to rule that school by love, and concluded by saying, "I want to ask you one favor – that is, if you love me, try and be a good boy"; and I never gave her trouble again. She just put me under grace. And that is what the Lord does. God is love, and he wants us all to love Him.

Child Friendship How Durable

I heard some time ago of a little book upon a passage of Scripture, I didn't know there was such a passage; which occurred in the story of David and Mephibosheth. You know, one day Jonathan and David were together, and Jonathan said, "David, I want you to make a vow." I suppose it had been revealed to Jonathan that he was to take his place.

Instead of his heart being filled with jealousy, he loved him as a brother. "Now, I want you to make a vow that when you get my father's throne, if any of my father's house are alive, you will show them kindness."

"Why, yes, Jonathan," replies David; "I will. I would do it for your sake alone."

Well, time went on. You know how Saul persecuted David, and drove him into the cave of Adullam, and if he could have caught him, you know how he would have slain him. News came to him that the Israelites were routed, and that Saul and Jonathan were slain, and David came up to Hebron, and reigned for seven and a half years, and came after this up to Jerusalem.

I can see him in his palace in the height of his power, and the recollection of the old vow he made to Jonathan suddenly comes upon him. His conscience tells him he has made a vow to his old friend Jonathan which he has not kept. I can see him order in one of his servants, "Do you know if there are any of Saul's house alive?"

"Well, I don't know, but there is an old servant of Saul's, Ziba."

David orders him in, and asks, "Are any of Saul's house alive, because if there are I want to show kindness to them."

I can imagine the expression of his face. The idea of David showing kindness to any of Saul's house; to Saul, who wanted to slay him and who persecuted him.

"Well, yes," the servant answers; "there is a son of Jonathan living."

"What!" he cries; "a son of my old friend Jonathan; where is he?"

"He was at Lo-debar the last I heard of him."

Now, you may have been a great traveler, and yet you have never heard of Lo-debar. You may have been all around the world, and still you have not heard of Lo-debar. You may work in the post office, and you have never heard of Lo-debar;

never saw a letter directed to that place. Still, that is the place where every one of Adam's sons has been. Every one has been in Lo-debar. Every backslider is there.

When David heard where he was, he sent down to bring up Jonathan's son, Mephibosheth. See that chariot sweeping through the town. "Why, the king's chariot is here," the people say; "what does it mean?"

We are told that this poor prince was lame, and I can see the poor, lame prince as he comes out to meet the servant. "What is it?" he inquires. "King David has sent for you," the servant replies. I can see the prince trembling from head to foot when he hears this. He thinks King David wants to slay him; he thinks he is just going to cut off his head. That's the way with sinners. They think that God stands behind them with a double-whetted sword ready to annihilate them.

The servant says, "I want you to come down and see the king."

"But," replies the prince, "I tell you that means death to me." Just as a good many sinners think.

"But," continues the servant, "he has sent me, and wants you to come;" and he gets him into the carriage and onto the highway, through the streets and unto the palace of the king.

The king looks upon him, and sees upon his brow the image of Jonathan, and says to Mephibosheth, "I will show thee kindness for thy father's sake, and I will restore unto you all of Saul's possessions, and you shall sit at the king's table." He restores to the lame prince the inheritance he lost, and then gives him a place at the king's table. That is the gospel. God wants you to come up from Lo-debar to Jerusalem and take your inheritance. The moment you come from your Lo-debar to the city of peace, that moment you will learn the glad tidings.

The Blind Child

I was in an infirmary not long since, and a mother brought a little child in. She said, "Doctor, my little child's eyes have not been opened for several days, and I would just like you to do something for them."

The doctor got some ointment and put it first on one and then on the other, and just pulled them open. "Your child is blind," said the doctor; "perfectly blind; it will never see again."

At first the mother couldn't take it in, but after a little she cast an appealing look upon that physician, and in a voice full of emotion, said, "Doctor, you don't mean to say that my child will never see again?"

"Yes," replied the doctor; "your child has lost his sight and will never see again."

And that mother just gave a scream, and drew that child to her bosom. "Oh, my darling child," sobbed the woman; "are you never to see the mother that gave you birth; never to see the world again?"

I could not keep back the tears when I saw the terrible agony of that woman when she realized the misfortune that had come upon her child. That was a terrible calamity, to grope in total darkness through this world; never to look upon the bright sky, the green fields; never to see the faces of loved ones; but what was it in comparison to the loss of a soul? I would rather have my eyes plucked out of my head and go down to my grave in total blindness, than lose my soul.

A Little Boy Converts his Mother

I remember, when on the North Side, I tried to reach a family time and again and failed. One night in the meeting, I noticed one of the little boys of that family. He hadn't come for any good, however; he was sticking pins in the backs of the other boys. I thought if I could get hold of him it would do good.

I used always to go to the door and shake hands with the boys, and when I got to the door and saw this little boy coming out, I shook hands with him and patted him on the head, and said I was glad to see him and hoped he would come again. He hung his head and went away.

The next night, however, he came back, and he behaved better than he did the previous night. He came two or three times after, and then asked us to pray for him that he might become a Christian. That was a happy night for me. He became a Christian, and a good one.

One night I saw him weeping. I wondered if his old temper had got hold of him again, and when he got up I wondered what he was going to say. "I wish you would pray for my mother," he said. When the meeting was over I went to him, and asked, "Have you ever spoken to your mother, or tried to pray with her?"

"Well, you know, Mr. Moody," he replied, "I never had an opportunity; she don't believe, and won't hear me."

"Now," I said, "I want you to talk to your mother tonight." For years I had been trying to reach her and couldn't do it.

So, I urged him to talk to her that night, and I said, "I will pray for you both."

When he got to the sitting room he found some people there, and he sat waiting for an opportunity, when his mother said it was time for him to go to bed. He went to the door undecided. He took a step, stopped, and turned around and hesitated for a minute, then ran to his mother and threw his arms around her neck and buried his face in her bosom. "What is the matter?" she asked; she thought he was sick.

Between his sobs he told his mother how for five weeks he had wanted to be a Christian; how he had stopped swearing; how he was trying to be obedient to her, and how happy he would be if she would be a Christian, and then went off to bed. She sat for a few minutes, but couldn't stand it, and went up to his room.

When she got to the door she heard him weeping, and praying, "Oh God, convert my dear mother." She came down again but couldn't sleep that night.

Next day she told the boy to go and ask Mr. Moody to come over and see her. He called at my place of business (I was in business then), and I went over as quiet as I could. I found her sitting in a rocking chair weeping. "Mr. Moody," she said, "I want to become a Christian."

"What has brought that change over you? I thought you didn't believe in it." Then she told me how her boy had come to her, and how she hadn't slept any all night, and how her sin rose up before her like a dark mountain. The next Sunday that boy came and led that mother into the Sabbath school, and she became a Christian worker.

Oh, little children, if you find Christ, tell it to your fathers and mothers. Throw your arms around their necks and lead them to Jesus.

Sympathy

I want to tell you a lesson taught me in Chicago a few years ago. In the months of July and August, a great many deaths occurred among children, you all know. I remember I attended a great many funerals; sometimes I would go to two or three funerals a day. I got so used to it that it did not trouble me to see a mother take the last kiss, and the last look at her child, and see the coffin lid closed. I got accustomed to it, as in the war we got accustomed to the great battles, and to see the wounded and the dead never troubled us.

When I got home one night, I heard that one of my Sunday school pupils was dead, and her mother wanted me to come to the house. I went to the poor home and saw the father drunk. Adelaide had been brought from the river. The mother told me she washed for a living, the father earned no money, and poor Adelaide's work was to get wood for the fire.

She had gone to the river that day and seen a piece floating on the water, had stretched out for it, had lost her balance, and fallen in. The poor woman was very much distressed. "I would like you to help me, Mr. Moody," she said, "to bury my child. I have no lot, I have no money."

Well, I took the measure for the coffin and came away. I had my little girl with me, and she said, "Papa, suppose we were very, very poor, and mamma had to work for a living, and I had to get sticks for the fire, and was to fall into the river, would you be very sorry?"

This question reached my heart. "Why, my child, it would break my heart to lose you," I said, and I drew her to my bosom.

"Papa, do you feel bad for that mother?" she said. This word woke my sympathy for the woman, and I started and went back to the house, and prayed that the Lord might bind up that wounded heart.

When the day came for the funeral, I went to Graceland. I had always thought my time too precious to go out there, but I went. The drunken father was there and the poor mother. I bought a lot, the grave was dug, and the child laid among strangers.

There was another funeral coming up, and the corpse was laid near the grave of little Adelaide. And I thought how I would feel if it had been my little girl that I had been laying there among strangers. I went to my Sabbath school thinking this and suggested that the children should contribute and buy a lot, in which we might bury a hundred poor little children.

We soon got it, and the papers had scarcely been made out, when a lady came and said, "Mr. Moody, my little girl died this morning; let me bury her in the lot you have got for the Sunday school children." The request was granted, and she asked me to go to the lot and say prayers over her child. I went to the grave; it was a beautiful day in June, and I remember asking her what the name of her child was. She said Emma. That was the name of my little girl, and I thought what if it had been my own child.

We should put ourselves in the places of others. I could not help shedding a tear. Another woman came shortly after and wanted to put another one into the grave. I asked his name. It was Willie, and it happened to be the name of my little boy; the first two laid there were called by the same names as my two children, and I felt sympathy and compassion for those two women.

If you want to get into sympathy, put yourself into a man's

place. We need Christians whose hearts are full of compassion and sympathy. If we haven't got it, pray that we may have it, so that we may be able to reach those men and women that need kindly words and kindly actions far more than sermons. The mistake is, that we have been preaching too much, and sympathizing too little. The gospel of Jesus Christ is a gospel of deeds and not of words.

A Boy's Story

Some years ago, as I was about to close a prayer meeting, a young man got up and urged all those men present that had not yet accepted of Christ, to do so that night. And in closing up his little speech, he said, "I once had a father and mother that cared more for my soul than for anything else. At last my father died; and when my father was dead and gone, my mother was more anxious than ever for me, and sometimes she would come and put her loving arms around my neck, and she would just plead with me to go to Christ.

"She used to tell me, after my father was dead, that she was lonesome without having me a Christian. I told her I sympathized with her; but declared I wanted to see a little of the world. I did not want to become a Christian in early life.

"Sometimes I would wake up past midnight and would hear a voice in my mother's chamber. I would hear that godly mother crying to God for her boy. I was her only child. I was very dear to her. At last I felt I must either become a Christian or go away from that mother's influence; and I ran away.

"After I had been gone a long time, I heard from home indirectly. I heard my mother was sick. I knew what it meant. I knew that she was pining for me. I knew her heart was broken on account of me and my wayward life. I thought I would go home and ask my mother to forgive me. My second thought was, if I did, I would have to go and be a Christian. I could not stay under the same roof without becoming a Christian.

" My rebellious heart said, 'I will not go.' When I heard again, I heard my mother was much worse. The thought came, supposing my mother should die, supposing I should never see that mother again, I never could forgive myself. I started for home. There was no train to my native village. I took the coach.

"I got in just after dark. The moon was shining. I had to go about a mile and a half to my mother's house; and on my way I thought I would go by the village graveyard, and I thought I would get over the fence, and go to the grave where my father was buried, to see if there was a new-made grave. It might be that mother was gone.

"When I drew near that grave, my heart began to beat more quickly, as by the light of the moon I saw the new-made grave. The whole story was told. The whole story was clear. My sainted mother was gone. It was a fresh-made grave. It had just been dug. For the first time in my life this question came stealing over me: Who was going to pray for my lost soul now? Father and mother both gone now. And, young men, I would have given the world, if I could have called that mother back and have her put her arms around my neck and heard her breathe my name in prayer. But her voice was silent forever. She was gone.

"I knelt beside that grave, crying that God might have mercy on me, and that God would forgive me. And I did not leave that grave all night till the morning dawn. But before morning I believed that God, for Christ's sake, had forgiven my sins, and that my mother's God had become my God. But, young men, I would never forgive myself. I never can. I killed that mother. I trampled her prayers and her entreaties under my feet. I broke her heart and sent her to her grave. Young man, if you have a godly mother, treat her kindly."

The Dying Sunday School Teacher

I want to tell how I got my first impulse to work solely for the conversion of men. For a long time after my conversion, I didn't accomplish anything. I hadn't got my right place. That was it. I hadn't thought enough of this personal work. I'd get up in prayer-meeting, and I'd pray with the others, but just to go up to a man and take hold of his coat and get him down on his knees, I hadn't yet got round to that.

It was in 1860 the change came. In the Sunday school I had a pale, delicate young man as one of the teachers. I knew his burning piety and assigned him to the worst class in the school. They were all girls, and it was an awful class. They kept gadding around in the schoolroom and were laughing and carrying on all the while. And this young man had better success than anyone else.

One Sunday he was absent, and I tried myself to teach the class, but couldn't do anything with them; they seemed further off than ever from any concern about their souls. Well, the day after his absence, early Monday morning, the young man came into the store where I worked, and, tottering and bloodless, threw himself down on some boxes. "What's the matter?" I asked.

"I have been bleeding at the lungs, and they have given me up to die," he said.

"But you are not afraid to die?" I questioned.

"No," said he, "I am not afraid to die, but I have got to stand before God and give an account of my stewardship, and not one of my Sabbath school scholars has been brought to Jesus. I have failed to bring one, and haven't any strength to do it now."

He was so weighed down that I got a carriage and took that dying man in it, and we called at the homes of every one of his scholars, and to each one he said, as best his faint voice would let him, "I have come to just ask you to come to the Savior," and then he prayed as I never heard before.

And for ten days he labored in that way, sometimes walking to the nearest houses, and at the end of that ten days every one of that large class had yielded to the Savior. Full well do I remember the night before he went away (for the doctors said he must hurry to the south), how we held a true love-feast. It was the very gate of heaven, that meeting. He prayed, and they prayed; he didn't ask them, he didn't think they could pray; and then we sung, "Blest be the tie that binds."

It was a beautiful night in June that he left on the Michigan Southern, and I was down to the train to help him off. And those girls, every one, gathered there again, all unknown to each other; and the depot seemed a second gate to heaven, in the joyful, yet tearful communion and farewells between those newly redeemed souls and him whose crown of rejoicing it will be that he led them to Jesus. At last the gong sounded, and, supported on the platform, the dying man shook hands with each one and whispered, "I will meet you yonder."

Prayer Answered

Only a few years ago, in the city of Philadelphia, there was a mother who had two sons. They were just going as fast as they could to ruin. They were breaking her heart, and she went into a little prayer-meeting and got up and presented them for prayer. They had been on a drunken spree, or had just got started in that way, and she knew that their end would be a drunkard's grave, and she went among these Christians and said, "Won't you just cry to God for my two boys?"

The next morning those two boys had made an appointment to meet each other on the corner of Market and Thirteenth streets, though not that they knew anything about our meeting; and while one of them was there at the corner, waiting for his brother to come, he followed the people who were flooding into the depot building, and the spirit of the Lord met him, and he was wounded and found his way to Christ.

After his brother came, he found the place too crowded to enter, so he too went curiously into another meeting and found Christ, and went home happy; and when he got home he told his mother what the Lord had done for him, and the second son came with the same tidings. I heard one of them get up afterwards to tell his experience in the young converts' meeting, and he had no sooner told the story than the other got up and said, "I am that brother, and there is not a happier home in Philadelphia than we have got."

The Smiling Child

In London, in 1872, one Sunday morning a minister said to me, "I want you to notice that family there in one of the front seats, and when we go home I want to tell you their story." When we got home I asked him for the story, and he said, "All that family were won by a smile."

"Why," said I, "how's that?"

"Well," said he, "as I was walking down a street one day, I saw a child at a window; it smiled, and I smiled, and we bowed. So it was the second time; I bowed, she bowed. It was not long before there was another child, and I had got in a habit of looking and bowing, and pretty soon the group grew, and at last, as I went by, a lady was with them. I didn't know what to do. I didn't want to bow to her, but I knew the children expected it, and so I bowed to them all. And the mother saw I was a minister, because I carried a Bible every Sunday morning.

"So, the children followed me the next Sunday and found I was a minister. And they thought I was the greatest preacher and their parents must hear me. A minister who is kind to a child and gives him a pat on the head, why, the children will think he is the greatest preacher in the world. Kindness goes a great way. And to make a long story short, the father and mother and five children were converted, and they are going to join our church next Sunday."

Won to Christ by a smile! We must get the wrinkles out of our brows, and we must have smiling faces.

The Stolen Boy

There was a boy a great many years ago, stolen in London, the same as Charley Ross was stolen here. Long months and years passed away, and the mother had prayed and prayed, as the mother of Charley Ross has prayed, I suppose, and all her efforts had failed, and they had given up all hope; but the mother did not quite give up her hope.

One day a little boy was sent up into the neighboring house to sweep the chimney, and by some mistake he got down again through the wrong chimney. When he came down, he came in by the sitting room chimney. His memory began at once to travel back through the years that had passed. He thought that things looked familiar. The scenes of the early days of youth were dawning upon him; and as he stood there surveying the place, his mother came into the room. He stood there covered with rags and soot.

Did she wait until she sent him to be washed before she rushed and took him in her arms? No, indeed; it was her own boy. She took him to her arms, all black and smoke, and hugged him to her bosom, and shed tears of joy upon his head.

Little Jimmy

A friend of mine in Chicago took his Sabbath school out on the cars once. A little boy was allowed to sit on the platform of the car, when by some mischance he fell, and the whole train passed over him. They had to go on half a mile before they could stop. They went back to him and found that the poor little fellow had been cut and mangled all to pieces.

Two of the teachers went back with the remains to Chicago. Then came the terrible task of telling the parents about it. When they got to the house they dared not go in. They were waiting there for five minutes before anyone had the courage to tell the story. But at last they ventured in.

They found the family at dinner. The father was called out; they thought they would tell the father first. He came out with the napkin in his hand. My friend said to him, "I have got very bad news to tell you. Your little Jimmy has got run over by the cars."

The poor man turned deathly pale and rushed into the room, crying out, "Dead, dead." The mother sprang to her feet and came out of the sitting room to where the teachers were. When she heard the sad story, she fainted dead away at their feet.

"Mr. Moody," said my friend, "I wouldn't be the messenger of such tidings again if you would give me the whole of Chicago. I never suffered so much. I have got a son dearer to me than my life, and yet I would rather have a train a mile long run over him than that he should die without God and without hope." What is the loss of a child to the loss of a soul?

Willie

A short time after I got here, I received a letter from Scotland. It was sent to a minister, and he forwarded it to me. It was the gushing of a loving father. He asked us to look out for his boy, whose name was Willie. That name touched my heart, because it was the name of my own boy.

I asked Mr. Sawyer to try and get on the track of that boy some weeks ago, but all his efforts were fruitless. But away off in Scotland that Christian father was holding that boy up to God in prayer, and last Friday, in yonder room, among those asking for prayers was that Willie, and he told me a story there that thrilled my heart, and testified how the prayers of that father and mother in that far-off land had been instrumental in effecting his salvation.

Don't you think the heart of that father and mother will rejoice? He said he was rushing madly to destruction, but there was a power in those prayers that saved that boy. Don't you think, my friends, that God hears and answers prayers, and shall we not lift up our voices to Him in prayer that He will bless the children He has given us?

The Child & the Book

I like to think of Christ as a burden-bearer. A minister was one day moving his library upstairs. As the minister was going upstairs with his load of books, his little boy came in and was very anxious to help his father. So, his father just told him to go and get an armful and take them upstairs.

When the father came back, he met the little fellow about half-way up the stairs, tugging away with the biggest in the library. He couldn't manage to carry it up. The book was too big. So he sat down and cried. His father found him, and just took him in his arms, book and all, and carried him upstairs. So Christ will carry you and all your burdens.

Breaking the Tumblers

A lady once told me she was in her pantry on one occasion, and she was surprised by the ringing of a bell. As she whirled around to see what it was, she broke a tumbler. Her little child was standing there, and she thought her mother was doing a very correct thing, and the moment the lady left the pantry, the child commenced to break all the tumblers she could get hold of. You may laugh, but children are very good imitators.

If you don't want them to break the Sabbath day, keep it holy yourself. It is very often by imitation that they utter their first oath; that they tell their first lie, and it grows upon them, and when they try to quit the habit, it has grown so strong upon them that they cannot do it.

The Recitation

I heard of a Sunday school concert at which a little child of eight was going to recite. Her mother had taught her, and when the night came the little thing was trembling so she could scarcely speak.

She commenced, "Jesus said," and completely broke down. Again she tried it, "Jesus said suffer," but she stopped once more. A third attempt was made by her, "Suffer little children, and don't anybody stop them, for He wants them all to come," and that is the truth.

There is not a child who has a parent in this church that He doesn't want, and if you but bring them in the arms of your faith, and ask the Son of God to bless them and train them in the knowledge of God, and teach them as you walk your way, as you lie down at night, as you rise up in the morning, they will be blessed.

How Little Moody Took the Whippings

When I was a boy, my mother used to send me outdoors to get a birch stick to whip me with; and at first, I used to stand off from the rod as far as I could. But I soon found that the whipping hurt me more that way than any other; and so I went as near to my mother as I could and found the punishment lighter. And so when God chastens us, let us kiss the rod and draw as near to Him as we can.

Someone has said that God sent one son into the world without sin, but no son without sorrow. We are not able to read the problem now, or to see just why we are affected; but by-and-by we shall know, and all will be made plain.

There is one passage of Scripture which has always been a great comfort to me. In the eighth chapter of Romans, Paul says, "All things work together for good to them that love God."

A few years ago, a little child of mine had the scarlet fever; and I went to the druggist to get the prescription which the doctor had ordered, and told him to be sure and be very careful in making it up. And the druggist took down one bottle after another, in any one of which there might be what would be rank poison for my child; but he stirred them together and mixed them up, and made just the medicine which my child needed; and so God gives us a little adversity here, a little prosperity there, and works all for our good.

Dr. Chalmers' Story

There is a story of Dr. Chalmers. A lady came to him, and said, "Doctor, I cannot bring my child to Christ. I've talked, and talked, but it's of no use."

The doctor thought she had not much skill, and said, "Now, you be quiet, and I will talk to her alone." When the doctor got the Scotch lassie alone he said to her, "They are bothering you a good deal about this question; now, suppose I just tell your mother you don't want to be talked to any more upon this subject for a year. How will that do?"

Well, the Scotch lassie hesitated a little, and then said she didn't think it would be safe to wait for a year. Something might turn up. She might die before then. "Well, that's so," replied the doctor, "but suppose we say six months."

She didn't think even this would be safe. "That's so," was the doctor's reply; "well, let us say three months."

After a little hesitation, the girl finally said, "I don't think it would be safe to put it off for three months; don't think it would be safe to put it off at all," and they went down on their knees and found Christ.

Over the Mountains

A lady had a little child that was dying. She thought it was resting sweetly in the arms of Jesus. She went into the room, and the child asked her, "What are those clouds and mountains that I see so dark?"

"Why, Eddy," said his mother, "there are no clouds or mountains; you must be mistaken."

"Why, yes, I see great mountains, and dark clouds, and I want you to take me in your arms and carry me over the mountains."

"Ah," said the mother, "you must pray to Jesus; He will carry you safely."

And, my friends, the sainted mother, the praying wife, may come to your bedside and wipe the damp sweat from your brow, but they cannot carry you over the Jordan when the hour comes.

This mother said to her little boy, "I am afraid that it is unbelief that is coming upon you, my child, and you must pray that the Lord will be with you in your dying moments."

And the two prayed, but the boy turned to her, and said, "Don't you hear the angels, mother, over the mountains and calling for me, and I cannot go?"

"My dear boy, pray to Jesus, and He will come; He only can take you."

And the boy closed his eyes and prayed, and when he opened them a heavenly smile overspread his face, as he said, "Jesus has come to carry me over the mountains."

Dear sinner, Jesus is ready and willing to carry you over the mountains of sin, and over your mountains of unbelief. Give yourself to Him.

The Smiling Mother's Sad Farewell

A few years ago, I was in a town in our state, the guest of a family that had a little boy about thirteen years, who did not bear the family name, yet was treated like the rest. Every night when he retired, the lady of the house kissed him and treated him in every respect like all the other children.

I said to the lady of the house, "I don't understand it." I think he was the finest looking boy I have ever seen. I said to her, "I don't understand it."

She says, "I want to tell you about that boy. That boy is the son of a missionary. His father and mother were missionaries in India, but they found they had to bring their children back to this country to educate them. So, they gave up their mission field, and came back to educate their children, and to find some missionary work to do in this country.

But they were not prospered here as they had been in India, and the father said, "I will go back to India"; and the mother said, "If God has called you to go, I am sure it will be my duty to go and my privilege to go, and I will go with you."

The father said, "You have never been separated from the children, and it will be hard for you to be separated from them; perhaps you had better stay and take care of them."

But after prayer they decided to leave their children to be educated, and they left for India. This lady heard of it and sent a letter to the parents, in which she stated if they left one child at her house, she would treat it like one of her own children.

She said the mother came and spent a few days at her house, and, being satisfied that her boy would receive proper care, consented to leave him, and the night before she was to leave him, the missionary said to the western lady, "I want to leave my boy tomorrow morning without a tear"; said she, "I may never see him again." But she didn't want him to think she was weeping for anything she was doing for the Master.

The lady said to herself, "She won't leave that boy without a tear." But the next day when the carriage drove up to the door, the lady went upstairs, and she heard the mother crying in prayer, "Oh God, give me strength for this hour. Help me to go away from my boy without a tear."

When she came down there was a smile upon her face. She hugged him and she kissed him, but she smiled as she did it. She gave up all her five or six children without shedding a tear, went back to India, and in about a year there came a voice, "Come up hither." Do you think she would be a stranger in the Lord's world? Don't you think she will be known there as a mother that loved her child?

Off for America

Previous to my coming across to this great country of ours, I was holding meetings in London. I took my ticket from there to Manchester to bid some friends good-bye.

When I got to the railway carriage I saw little groups of boys around two little fellows. Their coats were threadbare, with patches here and there carefully covering up the holes. Some good mother, it was evident, too poor to send them away in fine style, was trying to make them as neat as she could.

The boys belonged to a Sunday school in London, and the group around them were their school-mates, who had come down to bid them good-bye. They shook hands, and then their Sunday-school teacher did the same and wished them godspeed. After that, their minister came and took them by the hand and breathed a prayer that they would be blessed.

When they all had bade the boys good-bye, a poor widow came up and put her arm around the companion of her son. Perhaps he had no mother, and she kissed him for his mother, and wished him good-bye. Then she put her arms around the neck of the other boy, and he put his arms around her, and she began to weep. "Don't cry, mother," said the boy, "don't cry; I'll soon be in America, and I'll save money, and soon send for you to come out to me; I'll have you out with me. Don't cry."

He stepped into the carriage, the steam was turned on, and the train was in motion when he put his head out of the window, and cried, "Farewell, dear mother"; and the mother's prayer went out, "God bless my boy, God bless my boy."

Don't you think that when they came to America, and sent the first letter to England, that mother would run quickly to the door when the postman came with that letter? How quick that mother would take that letter and break the seal! She wants to hear good news. There is not one here who has not a message of good news, of glad tidings; better news than was ever received by a mother in England from a son in America, or from a mother in England by a son in America. It is glad tidings from a loving Savior; glad tidings of great joy.

Parting Words

But I have another story to tell. It was Ralph Wallace who told me of this one. A certain gentleman was a member of the Presbyterian church. His little boy was sick.

When he went home, his wife was weeping, and she said, "Our boy is dying; he has had a change for the worse. I wish you would go in and see him." The father went into the room and placed his hand upon the brow of his dying boy, and could feel the cold, damp sweat was gathering there; that the cold, icy hand of death was feeling for the chords of life.

"Do you know, my boy, that you are dying?" asked the father.

"Am I? Is this death? Do you really think I am dying?"

"Yes, my son, your end on earth is near."

"And will I be with Jesus tonight, father?"

"Yes, you will be with the Savior."

"Father, don't you weep, for when I get there I will go straight to Jesus and tell Him that you have been trying all my life to lead me to Him."

God has given me two little children, and ever since I can remember, I have directed them to Christ, and I would rather they carried this message to Jesus, that I had tried all my life to lead them to Him, than have all the crowns of the earth; and I would rather lead them to Jesus than give them the wealth of the world. I challenge any man to speak of heaven without speaking of children. "For of such is the kingdom of heaven."

Moody and the Children

The first two or three years that I attempted to talk in the meetings, I saw that the older people did not like it. I had sense enough to know that I was a bore to them. Well, I went out upon the street and I got eighteen little children to follow me the first Sunday, and I led them into the Sunday-school.

I found that I had something to do. I was encouraged, and I kept at that work. And if I am worth anything to the Christian church today, it is as much due to that work as anything else. I could not explain these Scriptural passages to them, for I did not then comprehend them, but I could tell them stories; I could tell them that Christ loved them, and that He died for them. I did the best I could. I used the little talent I had, and God kept giving me more talents, and so, let me say, find some work.

See if you can get a Sabbath school to teach. If you cannot get that, go down into the dark lanes and byways of the city and talk to them and sing some gospel hymns; or, if you cannot sing, take someone with you that can sing some of these songs of praise. Sing or read the twenty-third psalm, or pray, and you can get a blessing in that way. When you have won one soul to Christ, you will want to win two, and when you get into the luxury of winning souls it will be a new world to you, and you will not think of going back to the world at all.

The Drunken Boy Reclaimed

Not long ago a young man went home late. He had been in the habit of going home late, and the father began to wonder if he had gone astray. He told his wife to go to bed, and dismissed the servants, and said he would sit up till his son came home.

The boy came home drunk, and the father in his anger gave him a push into the street, told him never to enter his house again, and shut the door. He went into the parlor and sat down, and began to think, "Well, I may be to blame for that boy's conduct after all. I have never prayed with him. I have never warned him of the dangers of the world." And the result of his reflections was that he put on his overcoat and hat and started out to find his boy.

The first policeman he met he asked eagerly, "Have you seen my boy?"

"No."

On he went till he met another. "Have you seen anything of my son?" He ran from one to another all that night, but not until the morning did he find him. He took him by the arm and led him home and kept him till he was sober.

Then he said, "My dear boy, I want you to forgive me; I've never prayed for you; I've never lifted up my heart to God for you; I've been the means of leading you astray, and I want your forgiveness." The boy was touched, and what was the result? Within twenty-four hours that son became a convert and gave up that cup.

The Fatal Slumber

There is a little story that has gone the round of the American press that made a great impression upon me as a father. A father took his little child out into the field one Sabbath, and, it being a hot day, he lay down under a beautiful, shady tree. The little child ran about gathering wild flowers and little blades of grass, and coming to its father and saying, "Pretty, pretty!"

At last the father fell asleep, and while he was sleeping, the little child wandered away. When he awoke, his first thought was, "Where is my child?" He looked all around, but he could not see it. He shouted at the top of his voice, but all he heard was the echo of his own voice. Running to a little hill, he looked around and shouted again.

No response! Then going to a precipice at some distance, he looked down, and there, upon the rocks and briars, he saw the mangled form of his loved child. While he was sleeping his child had wandered over the precipice. I thought, as I heard that, what a sad picture of the church of God!

How many fathers and mothers, how many Christian men, are sleeping now while their children wander over the terrible precipice right into the bottomless pit. Father, where is your boy tonight?

Open the Door

I heard of a little child, some time ago, who was burned. The mother had gone out and left the three children at home. The eldest left the room, and the remaining two began to play with fire and set the place in a blaze.

When the youngest of the two saw what she had done, she went into a little cupboard and fastened herself in. The remaining child went to the door and knocked and knocked, crying to her to open the door and let her take her out of the burning building, but she was too frightened to do it.

It seems to me as if this was the way with hundreds and thousands. Christ stands and knocks, but they've got their hearts barred and bolted, because they don't know that He has come only to bless them.

Obedience Explained

Suppose I say to my boy, "Willie, I want you to go out and bring me a glass of water." He says he doesn't want to go.

"I didn't ask you whether you wanted to go or not, Willie; I told you to go."

"But I don't want to go," he says.

"I tell you, you must go and get me a glass of water."

He does not like to go. But he knows I am very fond of grapes, and he is very fond of them himself, so he goes out, and someone gives him a beautiful cluster of grapes.

He comes in and says, "Here, papa; here is a beautiful cluster of grapes for you."

"But what about the water?"

"Won't the grapes be acceptable, papa?"

"No, my boy, the grapes are not acceptable; I won't take them; I want you to get me a glass of water."

The little fellow doesn't want to get the water, but he goes out, and this time someone gives him an orange. He brings it in and places it before me. "Is that acceptable?" he asks.

"No, no, no!" I say, "I want nothing but water; you cannot do anything to please me until you get the water."

And so, my friends, to please God you must first obey Him.

The Little Bird's Freedom

A friend in Ireland once met a little Irish boy who had caught a sparrow. The poor little bird was trembling in his hand and seemed very anxious to escape. The gentleman begged the boy to let it go, as the bird could not do him any good; but the boy said he would not, for he had chased it three hours before he could catch it.

He tried to reason it out with the boy, but in vain. At last he offered to buy the bird; the boy agreed to the price, and it was paid.

Then the gentleman took the poor little thing and held it out in his hand. The boy had been holding it very fast, for the boy was stronger than the bird, just as Satan is stronger than we, and there it sat for a time, scarcely able to realize the fact that it had got liberty; but in a little while it flew away, chirping, as if to say to the gentleman, "Thank you! thank you! you have redeemed me."

That is what redemption is – buying back and setting free. So Christ came back to break the fetters of sin, to open the prison doors, and set the sinner free. This is the good news, the gospel of Christ; "Ye are not redeemed with corruptible things, as silver and gold, but with the precious blood of Christ."

Over the River

A minister who had lost his child asked another minister to come and preach for him. He came and he told how he lived on one side of a river, and felt very little interest in the people on the other side, until his daughter was married and went over there to live, and then every morning he went to the window and looked over the river and felt very much concerned about that town and all the people there.

"Now," said he, "I think that as this child has crossed another river, heaven will be dearer to him than ever it has been before." Shall we not just let our hearts and affections be set on the other side of the river? It is but a step; it is but a vail; we shall soon be in the other world.

Willie Asks Pardon and Prays

My little boy, who has been in the habit of waking up every morning at six o'clock, an hour before I want to wake, woke up one morning at half past five, and his mother told him he must keep still for an hour and a half; and he kept making a noise, till at last his mother had to speak pretty quick to him, and when I woke up I found the little fellow sobbing.

I said, "Willie, what's the matter?" Well, he was pretty angry with his mother. He got out of bed and knelt down, and I said, "What are you going to do?"

"I'm going to say my prayers."

I told him God wouldn't hear his prayer while he was angry with his mother. If you bring your prayers to God and have aught against your brother, you need not pray.

Well, the little fellow went off upstairs, and by-and-by he went up and asked his mother to forgive him, and then he prayed and went off with a light heart and kept a light heart all day. Christ says, "You can get victory through Me." When the love of God is shed abroad in our hearts, how easy it is to speak kindly of those who hate us and speak contemptuously of us!

Waiting for Jesus

I remember seeing a story some time ago in print. It has been in the papers, but it will not hurt us to hear it again. A family in a southern city were stricken down with yellow fever. It was raging there, and there were very stringent sanitary rules. The moment anybody died, a cart went around and took the coffin away.

The father was taken sick and died and was buried; and the mother was at last stricken down. The neighbors were afraid of the plague, and none dared to go into the house. The mother had a little son and was anxious about her boy and afraid he would be neglected when she was called away, so she called the little fellow to her bedside and said, "My boy, I am going to leave you, but Jesus will come to you when I am gone."

The mother died, the cart came along, and she was laid in the grave. The neighbors would have liked to take the boy, but were afraid of the pestilence. He wandered about and finally started up to the place where they had laid his mother and sat down on the grave and wept himself to sleep.

Next morning, he awoke and realized his position, alone and hungry. A stranger came along and seeing the little fellow sitting on the ground, asked him what he was waiting for. The boy remembered what his mother had told him, and answered, "I am waiting for Jesus," and told him the whole story.

The man's heart was touched, tears trickled down his cheeks, and he said, "Jesus has sent me," to which the boy replied, "You have been a good while coming, sir." He was provided for. So it is with us. To wait for results, we might have courage and patience, and God will help us.

A Child's Request for Prayer

At the close of one of the afternoon meetings we had in the Berkeley street church a few weeks ago, a little child brought me a note. I put it in my pocket and read it when I got home. It was this, "Won't you pray that my mother may come home?"

On inquiry I found that she was a little waif, her father was dead, and that her mother had deserted her and gone out to San Francisco and had been gone over a year. Well, I must confess it kind of staggered me that they should pray that that mother might come back.

But this note has just been handed to me, "You will remember the little child who asked prayers for her mother to return home, having been absent a year. This mother has returned and was at the meeting with her little child on Friday night." The little child now wants us to pray that her dear mother may be converted.

Emma's New Muff

I remember one time my little girl was teasing her mother to get her a muff, and so one day her mother brought a muff home, and, although it was storming, she very naturally wanted to go out in order to try her new muff. So, she tried to get me to go out with her.

I went out with her, and I said, "Emma, better let me take your hand." She wanted to keep her hands in her muff, and so she refused to take my hand. Well, by-and-by she came to an icy place, her little feet slipped, and down she went.

When I helped her up, she said, "Papa, you may give me your little finger."

"No, my daughter, just take my hand."

"No, no, papa, give me your little finger." Well, I gave my finger to her, and for a little way she got along nicely, but pretty soon we came to another icy place, and again she fell. This time she hurt herself a little, and she said, "Papa, give me your hand," and I gave her my hand, and closed my fingers about her wrist, and held her up so that she could not fall. Just so God is our keeper. He is wiser than we.

Pull for the Shore Sailor

A vessel was wrecked off the shore. Eager eyes were watching and strong arms manned the life boat. For hours they tried to reach that vessel through the great breakers that raged and foamed on the sand bank, but it seemed impossible.

The boat appeared to be leaving the crew to perish. But after a while the captain and sixteen men were taken off, and the vessel went down. "When the life boat came to you," said a friend, "did you expect it had brought some tools to repair your old ship?"

"Oh, no," was the response; "she was a total wreck. Two of her masts were gone, and if we had stayed mending her, only a few minutes, we must have gone down, sir."

"When once off the old wreck, and safe in the life boat, what remained for you to do?"

"Nothing, sir, but just to pull for the shore."

> Light in the darkness, sailor, day is at hand!
>   See o'er the foaming billows fair haven's land,
> Drear was the voyage, sailor, now almost o'er,
>   Safe within the life-boat, sailor, pull for the shore.
>
> CHO. – Pull for the shore, sailor, pull for the shore!
>   Heed not the rolling waves, but bend to the oar;
> Safe in the life-boat, sailor, cling to self no more!
>   Leave the poor old stranded wreck, and pull for the shore.

Trust in the life-boat, sailor, all else will fail,
　　Stronger the surges dash and fiercer the gale,
Heed not the stormy winds, though loudly they roar;
　　Watch the "bright morning star," and pull for the
　　　　shore. – CHO.

Bright gleams the morning, sailor, lift up thy eye;
　　Clouds and darkness disappearing, glory is nigh!
Safe in the life-boat, sailor, sing evermore;
　　"Glory, glory, hallelujah!" pull for the shore. – CHO.
　　　　P. P. Bliss.

Young Moody in Boston

I remember when I was a boy and went to Boston, I went to the post office two or three times a day to see if there was a letter for me. I knew there was not, as there was but one mail a day. I had not any employment, and was very homesick, and so I went constantly to the post office, thinking perhaps when the mail did come in, my letter had been mislaid.

At last, however, I got a letter. It was from my youngest sister, the first letter she ever wrote to me. I opened it with a light heart, thinking there was some good news from home, but the burden of the whole letter was that she had heard there were pickpockets in Boston, and warned me to take care of them.

I thought I had better get some money in hand first, and

then I might take care of pickpockets. And so you must take care to remember salvation is a gift. You don't work for salvation, but work day and night after you have got it.

Dinna Ye Hear Them Coming

There is a story told of an incident that occurred during the last Indian mutiny. The English were besieged in the city of Lucknow and were in momentary expectation of perishing at the hands of the fiends that surrounded them.

There was a little Scotch lassie in this fort, and, while lying on the ground, she suddenly shouted, her face aglow with joy, "Dinna ye hear them comin'? Dinna ye hear them comin'?"

"Hear what?" they asked.

"Dinna ye hear them comin'?" And she sprang to her feet. It was the bagpipes of her native Scotland she heard. It was a native air she heard that was played by a regiment of her countrymen marching to the relief of those captives, and these deliverers made them free. Oh my friends, don't you hear Jesus Christ crying to you tonight?

The Mistake that was Corrected

When we were in Great Britain, in Manchester, a father woke up to the fact that we were going away from that town. Just as we were about closing, he got wonderfully interested in the meetings, and when we had gone to another town he said to his wife, "I have made a mistake; I should have taken you and the children and the servants to those meetings. Now, I'm going to take my son from business, and take you and the children and the servants to the town where they are being held now, and take a house and have you all attend the meetings."

He came and took a house and sat down determined to remain there till all had been blessed. I remember him coming to me one night, soon after arriving, and saying, "Mr. Moody, my wife has got converted; thank God for that. If I get nothing else I am well paid."

A few nights after he came in and said his son had become converted, and then told me one of the servants had been brought under the influence; and so he went on until the last day we were to be in that town arrived, and he came to me and said the last one of the family had yielded himself up to Christ, and went back to his native city rejoicing. When we were in London the father and son came up and assisted in the work, and I don't know a happier man in all Europe than that one.

Let the Lower Lights be Burning

A few years ago, at the mouth of Cleveland harbor, there were two lights, one at each side of the bay, called the upper and lower lights; and to enter the harbor safely by night, vessels must sight both of the lights. These western lakes are more dangerous sometimes than the great ocean.

One wild, stormy night, a steamer was trying to make her way into the harbor. The captain and pilot were anxiously watching for the lights. By-and-by the pilot was heard to say, "Do you see the lower light?"

"No," was the reply; "I fear we have passed them."

"Ah, there are the lights," said the pilot; "and they must be, from the bluff on which they stand, the upper lights. We have passed the lower lights and have lost our chance of getting into the harbor."

What was to be done? They looked back, and saw the dim outline of the lower lighthouse against the sky. The lights had gone out. "Can't you turn your head around?"

"No; the night is too wild for that. She won't answer to her helm."

The storm was so fearful that they could do nothing. They tried again to make for the harbor, but they crashed against the rocks and sank to the bottom. Very few escaped; the great majority found a watery grave. Why? Simply because the lower lights had gone out. Now, with us the upper lights are all right. Christ Himself is the upper light, and we are the lower lights, and the cry to us is, *keep the lower lights burning;* that is what we have to do. He will lead us safe to the sunlit shore of Canaan, where there is no more night.

> Brightly beams our Father's mercy
>   From His lighthouse ever more,
> But to us He gives the keeping
>   Of the lights along the shore.
>
>   CHO. – Let the lower lights be burning!
>   Send a gleam across the wave!
>   Some poor fainting, struggling seaman
>   You may rescue, you may save.
>
> Dark the night of sin has settled,
>   Loud and angry billows roar;
> Eager eyes are watching, longing,
>   For the lights along the shore. – CHO.
>
> Trim your feeble lamp, my brother;
>   Some poor seaman tempest-tossed,
> Trying now to make the harbor,
>   In the darkness may be lost. – CHO.
>   P. P. Bliss.

The Little Boy

I remember a mother that lay dying. She had been married the second time, and she had a boy that her second husband, this step-father, did not like, and his mother sent for me, and she said, "Now I am dying from consumption. I have been sick a long time, and since I have been lying here, I have neglected that boy. He has got into bad company, and he is very, very unkind, and he is given to swearing; and, Mr. Moody, I want you to promise me that when I am gone, and he has no one to take care of him, you will look after him."

I promised that I would. And soon after that mother died, and no sooner was she buried than that boy ran away and they did not know where he went to. The next Sunday I spoke to the children in my Sabbath school, and I asked them to look for him, and if they found him to let me know. And for some time I did not hear of him, but one day one of my scholars told me that the boy was a bell-boy in a certain hotel, and so I went there and I found him and talked with him.

I remember it perfectly well; it was the third of July. He had no father or mother, but a step-father who did not care for him; and as I spoke to him kindly about Christ and what He had done for him, and how He loved him, the tears trickled down his cheeks, and when I asked him if he wanted to know Christ, he told me he did, and a little boy that was with me got down upon his knees and prayed with him; and at night – it was the night before the "Fourth" – he went up upon the flat roof, and they were firing off cannon and sky-rockets, and there upon that roof at midnight, upon the top of that hotel, that boy was praying and calling upon God for light, for aid, and for comfort, and now he is an active Christian young man, and superintendent of a Sabbath school.

He was taken right up, and he has held on, and he is leading others to Christ. There is a work for you. Take these children by the hand and lead them to the cross of Christ. They can be gathered into our churches and be a blessing to the church of God.

Emma's Kiss

A gentleman one day came to my office for the purpose of getting me interested in a young man who had just got out of the penitentiary. "He says," said the gentleman, "he don't want to go to the office, but I want your permission to bring him in and introduce him," and I took him by the hand and told him I was glad to see him. I invited him up to my house, and when I took him into my family, I introduced him as a friend.

When my little daughter came into the room, I said, "Emma, this is papa's friend." And she went up and kissed him, and the man sobbed aloud.

After the child left the room, I said, "What is the matter?"

"Oh, sir;" he said, "I have not had a kiss for years. The last kiss I had was from my mother, and she was dying. I thought I would never have another one again." His heart was broken.

The Little Winner

A little girl only eleven years old once came to me in a Sunday school, and said, "Won't you please pray that God will make me a winner of souls?" I felt so proud of her, and my pride was justified, for she has become one of the best winners of souls in the country.

Oh, suppose she lives threescore years, and goes on winning four or five souls every year; at the end of her journey there will be three hundred souls on the way to glory. And how long will it be before that little company swells to a great army? Don't you see how that little mountain rill keeps swelling till it carries everything before it? Little trickling streams have run into it, till now, a mighty river, it has great cities on its banks, and the commerce of all nations floating on its waters.

So, when a single soul is won to Christ, you cannot see the result. A single one multiplies to a thousand, and that unto ten thousand. Perhaps a million shall be the fruit; we cannot tell. We only know that the Christian who has turned so many to righteousness shall indeed shine ever and ever.

Cherries

– The prodigal son got down very low, but he did not get down low enough to beg; he went to work.

– I've lived nearly forty years, and I've learned one thing if I've learned nothing else; that no man or woman who treats disrespectfully father or mother ever prospers.

– The most devoted love on earth is the love of a mother for her child; but what is it in comparison to God's love? Mothers "may forget, yet I will not forget thee," saith the Lord.

– When I was in England, my little girl said, "Papa, why don't those colored folks wash themselves white?" You might as well try to make yourselves pure and holy without the help of God.

– Someone has said there were thousands of men in that camp who knew that God *could* use them, but David was the only one who believed that God *would* use him. Said David, "Now, I will go."

– There are three thoughts that I have tried to bring out, that God is love; that His love is unchangeable; that His love is everlasting. The fourth thought is this, that His love is unfailing. Your love is not.

– A great many people wonder why it is that they don't prosper and are not blessed in the world. It is no wonder to me. The wonder is that God blesses them as He does. If I had a child in constant rebellion toward me, I wouldn't want that child to prosper until that spirit of rebellion would be swept away, because prosperity would ruin them.

– It seems to me after I am dead and gone, I would rather have a man come to my grave and drop a tear, and say, "Here lies the man who converted me; who brought me to the cross of Christ;" it seems to me I would rather have this than a column of pure gold reaching to the skies built in my honor. If a man wants to be useful, follow Christ.

The Story of Moody's Life

*From a Boyhood of Little Promise,
He Grows to Be a Power*

Dwight L. Moody was born on a little farm back of Northfield, Mass., Feb. 5, 1837. There was a large family, and the farm alone was not sufficient to afford subsistence. The elder Moody was forced to help out the small income by working with the trowel when building was brisk. He died, leaving a wife and seven children, on the 28th of May, 1814. In the morning of that day he was at his usual work, but feeling a pain in his side, caused by over-exertion, he went home to rest. About one o'clock in the afternoon he felt the pain suddenly increasing, staggered to the bed, fell upon his knees beside it, and in this posture of prayer death seized upon him, before anyone knew he was seriously ill.

All that was left to the widow for her support was the little home on the mountain side, with an acre or two of land; and even this was encumbered with debt. Of her seven children the eldest was but thirteen years of age; and a month after her husband's death another boy and girl were born.

Some of her worldly-wise neighbors advised her to give

away or bind out her children, all except the twin babies; but this she was determined not to do. God had endowed her with unusual strength both of body and mind, and, trusting in Him, she bravely lifted her burden of poverty and toil, and carried it patiently, hopefully, and at length cheerfully, until the little ones were able to help her bear it, and at last to fill her hands with plenty as she had also filled their hearts with love and care.

Her brothers, in Boston, helped her to pay the interest of the mortgage on her home, the eldest boys helped to take care of the little farm, the mother took care of the house and children, and God took care of them all.

Somebody has said; "When God wants to make a great man he begins by making a great woman," a remark eminently true in this case; for a careful study of the two characters will show that the best and strongest points about Moody were plainly enough inherited from his mother.

It may be that a man can come to distinction who has a vain selfish woman for his mother. "All things are possible with God," but in such case, you only need to go a step further back and find that he takes after his grandmother. Mrs. Moody belongs to the women of the heroic age in America. If she had been born a hundred years earlier, there would have been among her sons a Warren, or a Putnam.

She possessed that powerful physical organism by means of which the women of New England, in early days, were able to endure the toils and hardships of life in the wilderness. They helped their husbands to clear lands and fight Indians, besides doing their full share of work in taking care of the house and raising stalwart sons and buxom daughters to fill it. These women taught their children to "trust in God and fear nothing."

But the basis of their character was religion; not technical or theological religion, but that binding of soul to God which seeks to make him a partner in all business, as well as a hearer of all prayer. With such a nature, exercised and sanctified by sorrow, patience, and devotion, this woman was qualified to be the mother of such a son.

The boyhood of Moody was allied with poverty, hard work, and at times even hunger. When he was old enough to run errands, he was given a home by a neighboring farmer, who permitted him to attend school part of the time. He learned reading, writing, and ciphering, and much boyish mischief, and had admitted that as a boy he excelled in rough and tumble fighting.

Aside from a splendid loyalty and love for his widowed mother, there was nothing in young Moody's boyhood career to show any inclination toward piety. Although reared in a community near the scene of the famous religious awakening under Jonathan Edwards, 100 years before, it is not on record that Moody received any deep religious impression until he had grown to young manhood. As a boy he attended with his mother the Unitarian church in his native town. When he was 17 he picked up a few meager personal belongings and leaving home in quest of fortune and fame, went to Boston, where one of his brothers was a salesman in a small shoe store. He had an uncle in the same line of business, and as soon as he entered the city he sought a position in his uncle's store.

Young Moody rebelled against his relative's advice to go back to the farm, and finally his uncle took him in on condition that his nephew should be governed by his advice and should attend the Sunday school and services at Mount Vernon Congregational church. The boy performed his duties in the store acceptably, but for a time was careless in religious matters. The orthodox sermons that he heard from Sunday to Sunday went over his head, as he described it. His Sunday school teacher had better success with him, and there soon sprang up a bond of attachment between teacher and pupil. This teacher made a report to the church pastor on young Moody's prospects in the religious life as follows:

"He is very unlikely to become a Christian of clear and decided views of gospel truth, still less to fill any extended sphere of public usefulness."

In due time young Moody applied for membership in the church. The board of deacons questioned him on points of doctrine and found him so backward that they refused him admission, or at least, advised him to wait for six months or a year, until he was better grounded in the faith. It was while under this probationary discipline that Moody experienced the conversion that changed the whole trend of his nature and filled him with a passion for doing good to others, which became the guiding star of his life.

One day he went into the church of Dr. Kirk, a Congregational minister in Boston, and for the first time listened to an evangelical sermon. It had the effect of making him uncomfortable and he resolved not to go back. He felt that his heart had been laid bare, and he wondered who had told the preacher about him. Something induced him to go back the next Sunday, however, and the impression was renewed. His Sunday school teacher in the meantime had come to see young Moody at his place of business, and it was during a talk with this friend that he entered into the assurance of faith which was destined to make him a world power as a preacher and evangelist. At the end of twelve months from his first application, his name went upon the membership roll of the church.

His business career in Boston seemed destined to be a failure, and young Moody resolved to go to New York. He had no money and walked. In New York, he again failed to secure a foothold, and began to dream of the west.

He came to Chicago and soon was earning a good salary as a shoe salesman. It is said that he could sell more shoes than any two clerks in the store. One of his fellow clerks at this period says of Moody: "He would never sit down in the store to chat or read the paper, as other clerks did when there were no customers, but as soon as he had served one buyer he was on the look-out for another. If none appeared, he would start off to the hotels or depots, or walk the streets in search of one."

Mr. Moody's religious tendencies were even then exerting a strong influence upon him. He became a puritan in spirit, and eschewed the theater, billiards, cards, and dances as the enticements of the devil. He organized a debating society among his fellow clerks, and night after night the young men debated foreordination versus free will, and the slavery problem. Mr. Moody had joined the Plymouth Congregational church on the south side by letter, and he started trouble in that aristocratic congregation at once. He was filled with the desire to exhort and pray and would not be silenced. He hired four pews in the church and attempted to fill them with young men. He next applied for a place as teacher in the Sunday school, but was informed that pupils were needed more than teachers. The following Sunday, young Moody appeared with eighteen ragged urchins from the streets.

Moody continued to bring recruits into the Sunday school, and as soon as a class was organized, he handed it over to another teacher and started out after more, keeping on until he had filled the school. Still the field did not satisfy him, and he allied himself with one of the smaller Methodist churches, where he had a freer hand and was allowed to exercise evangelizing methods to the full. He conceived the idea of founding an independent mission on the north side and rented a deserted saloon building in Market Street in the locality known as "Little Hell." The first collection of boys he picked off the streets for a Sunday school class was a wonder. There was not a pair of shoes in the lot. The roll of names that the youngsters gave him to hand to the secretary contained the following:

Red Eye
Darby the Cobbler
Smikes
Billy Bucktooth
Greenhorn
Madden the Butcher
Indian
Jacky Candles
Black Stove Pipe
Old Man
Billy Blucannon
Rag Breeches Cadet

The new mission was no sooner started than Mr. Moody began digging in another of the city's slums. At the foot of the Lake Shore drive there was an area known as "The Sands," which was said to be worse than "Five Points" in New York or "Saint, Giles" in London. Crime was common and less open than in "Little Hell." It was murder after nightfall and debauchery in daylight. When Moody went into this slum to drum up pupils for his mission, he was hissed, derided, and threatened. He thrived on opposition and bribed the little children with sweets and trinkets to come to his school. He won the gutter-snipe children first, and then the men and women began coming to hear him preach.

In a few months he had the biggest congregation on the north side. Mayor Haines took an interest in the work and granted Moody permission to take his "Sands" congregation into the hall over the old North market. The hall was generally used for a dance Saturday nights, and there were no chairs. Early Sunday mornings, Moody would sweep out the sawdust and scrub up the tobacco and beer. He elected himself a finance committee to get some chairs. He went to John V. Farwell for help. Mr. Farwell went to the hall and found the school leaning up against the walls. He talked to the urchins and when he had finished, Mr. Moody nominated him for superintendent of the North Market Sunday school. He was elected, and from that time on the dry goods merchant helped Moody's work with his purse.

The "Little Hell" and the "Sands" Sunday school jumped from a membership of 150 to 1,000. Mr. Moody distributed sugar and provisions and Mr. Farwell brought clothing. The north side ministers began to protest that the work was irregular and interfered with the established Sunday schools. But it grew and prospered. For six years, the North Market Sunday school was a power in the north side slums and was constantly adding departments for education and usefulness.

It is related that Moody at this period was often in danger of his life. He was chased by denizens of the slums. Once he was caught by a man whose wife had been persuaded to empty a jug of whiskey into the street. There were a dozen desperadoes around him. He begged for a chance to pray before he should be killed. Telling of it afterward, Moody said that when he dropped on his knees he prayed harder than he ever did before. The crowd that was clamoring for his life was softened, and in twenty minutes he was allowed to go to his Sunday school and a large portion of the mob followed him. The leader, the man whose whiskey had been wasted, afterward became a teacher in the school.

Incidents in Mr. Moody's Early Sunday School Work in Chicago

It was in the old North Market hall that President Lincoln made his first and only Sunday school address. Mr. Lincoln was in the city, and Mr. Farwell conceived the idea that the ragged children would be pleased with a talk by the president. Mr. Lincoln was adverse to going, but finally consented. Mr. Farwell introduced the president of the United States to the motley crowd and said he would talk to them if they would take off their hats and be quiet. President Lincoln made a plain, old-fashioned address. Fort Sumter was fired on a few months later, and it is related that sixty of the unruly big boys of the school went to the front in response to Lincoln's first call for soldiers.

* * * *

Moody held a jubilee in an old rookery opposite Market Hall, on a certain thanksgiving night. The "old rookery" was none other than the ex-saloon, now Moody's prayer-room, a most forlorn and wretched place, dimly lighted, and with no fire, where thirty or forty children had assembled to hold a jubilee; every one of them bearing marks of poverty, if not of actual want.

Moody had appointed a kind of love-feast, at which every one was to tell what he was most thankful for.

One little fellow, who had no other relative in the world but a decrepit old grandfather, with whom he lived in the greatest poverty, had become a Christian some time before, and, like others of the children, was trying to do a little home-missionary work on his own account. When his turn came to tell what he was most thankful for, he said,

"There was that big fellow, 'Butcher Kilroy,' who acted so bad that nobody would have him, and he had to be turned out of one class after another, till I was afraid he would be turned out of the school. It took me a long time to get him to come, and I begged for him to stay. I used to pray to Jesus every day to give him a new heart, and I felt pretty sure He would if we didn't turn him out. By-and-by Butcher Kilroy began to want to be a Christian, and now he is converted; and that is what makes this Thanksgiving the happiest one in all my life."

Another desperate case, of a boy they found on The Sands. He was a sort of chief of a gang of gutter-snipes, who, partly because they admired him and partly because they were afraid of him, allowed him to be a perfect tyrant over them. It was a long time before they could get near enough to this young ruffian to speak to him; but even he at last was caught with the missionary sugar and invited to come to the mission school.

It was a cold day in February; but the only garment he had was a man's old overcoat, so ragged that it had to be stitched together around his body, giving him the appearance of being sewed up in a great dirty bag. A big pair of shoes, and papers wrapped around his legs, completed his winter costume. In this outfit he made his appearance on Sunday, at the door of the North Market School. Moody, catching sight of him, gave him his hand, pulled him in, and, marching with him the whole length of the room, gave him a place in a class, with the same kindness and attention he would have shown to the best dressed boy on the North Side.

At sight of this wretched waif, a stranger visiting the school was moved to tears. After the exercises were over, he took him to his house and gave him a full suit of clothes belonging to his own son.

The wild lad, thus civilized in appearance, continued to attend the school; and at length, one by one, brought all his followers with him. That lad is now a Christian gentleman, in receipt of a large salary, and superintendent of a Sunday school in one of our large cities.

Many were the exciting scenes through which Moody passed, as month after month he continued the work of visitation. Sometimes he was shamefully treated; and on more than one occasion he was actually in danger of becoming a martyr to the cause. One Sunday morning he was visiting families for the purpose of bringing their children to his school, when a powerful man, who had sworn to kill him, sprang upon him with a heavy club, before he knew he was in danger. It was a run for dear life. The Sands were in an uproar. Some cheered on their man, knowing if he caught him it would be all over with him; while those who were friendly dared not come to his rescue, for fear of his wrathful pursuer. But it was all lost labor, to drive Moody away from a place where there were any children whom he felt ought to come to his school. On this occasion, as on others, he escaped by being very swift-footed, but he was sore pressed by his enemy, who seemed really in hopes of putting an end to his labors by putting an end to his life. Not at all discouraged, he went back the next Sunday, and kept on going again and again, till at last his gentleness and patience disarmed his adversary, who gave him no further trouble.

In his explorations one Saturday evening, he found a jug of whiskey in a house, which the men had brought home to drink next day. They were all away from home; but Moody gave the women a rousing temperance lecture and persuaded them to let him empty the whiskey into the street. Early on Sunday afternoon he returned, as he had promised, to take the children with him whom the women had consented to send to his school. But the men of the house were lying in wait to give him a pounding. He had touched them at a tender point, and they thirsted for revenge. The situation was desperate. One of them had stepped between him and the door before he was aware of it, and all were about to pounce upon him, when Moody arrested proceedings on this wise,

"See here, now, my men, if you are going to whip me for spilling the whiskey, you might at least give me time to say my prayers."

So unusual a proposal attracted their attention, and they

agreed to let him pray before they thrashed him, thinking it would add just so much to their sport. Moody at once dropped upon his knees and began to pray. Such praying these rough fellows had never heard. At first, they were astonished, then they were interested, then they were softened; and when he had finished his prayer they gathered around him, gave him their hands, declared he was a good fellow, and in a few minutes Moody was triumphantly marching towards the North Market Hall, with all the children of the house at his heels.

No class of persons was neglected, except those who had no need of attention. The great majority of those people, whatever other qualifications they lacked for being saved, had at least this one – they were sinners. The worst as well as the best who came to the great school, or the little prayer-meeting, found Mr. Moody, or some of his workers, holding the door open for them, and inviting them to enter the kingdom of heaven.

No matter how repulsive the person might be, Moody was always ready to help him; he seemed to take the most interest in those who were most wretched and needy. Instances enough to fill volumes might be given of his successful work for those who had always been considered beyond the reach of grace and salvation.

Among the worst places in the field was a sailors' boarding-house, which was continually haunted by a rough, quarrelsome crowd. This place, vile and dangerous to the last degree, Moody and his friend ventured to enter. They were set upon and threatened with broken heads if they did not leave immediately; but remembering that "a soft answer turneth away wrath," they gently replied that they meant no harm, and, as proof of their kind intentions, offered to sing a song. This task, of course, fell to the lot of his friend; for Moody never could sing a note; and he immediately struck up the hymn commencing –

> "Oh how happy are they
> Who the Savior obey,
> And have laid up their treasures above!"

The crowd listened to the singing with evident enjoyment; it was better singing than they were accustomed to. When the hymn was finished, Moody followed with prayer. From that day, they were privileged characters in that house and were held in high respect by all the inmates. They captured the children of the keeper of the den for the North Market Mission, every one of whom was afterwards brought to Christ.

It was not often that their visits to saloons resulted so favorably as in the following case. Going into a drinking den one Saturday night, when the carousal was at its highest, they asked permission to leave some religious papers for the men who were drinking at the little tables around the room. This being done, they entered into conversation with the keeper of the place, and presently drew out the fact that his parents were Christian people. The question instantly followed, "Do they know you are selling liquor?"

The man hesitated and seemed deeply affected. They gave him a kindly word, and then bade him goodnight. But they had not gone far before one said to the other,

"We have neglected our duty; let us go back and pray with that man."

They immediately turned back, re-entered the saloon, begged the keeper's pardon for having neglected to pray with him, and, kneeling there in the sawdust, Moody offered a prayer which seemed the direct inspiration of the Holy Ghost. Mr. Moody's friend says,

"I never heard Moody pray like that before; it seemed as if the baptism of the Holy One was upon him."

Two weeks afterwards one of them met the man in the street,

who informed him that he had given up the saloon business, had left off drinking, and would die in the poor-house rather than sell any more liquor.

The most miserable of the many wretched families they met in all their visitation was one which they found one Sunday morning in an attic. The husband, who was just on the verge of *delirium tremens,* had become half idiotic from drink, while the wife and children were half dead from starvation. The first thing done was to give them something to eat. Next, they held a temperance meeting, and persuaded the man to sign the pledge, a copy of which they usually carried with them; and by way of impressing it upon his stupid senses, they made him kneel down and place his hand upon the pledge, while they prayed to God to give him strength to keep it. The next Sunday the whole family, decently clad, came to the mission school.

An evening or two afterwards, passing by the same house, the man hailed them from his attic window, and threw them down a piece of silver, saying "I believe in that Sunday school, and I want to take a little stock in it."

On Mr. Moody's friend returning to Chicago, six years afterwards, he was saluted by a gentlemanly stranger, who proved to be none other than the poor man who had thrown the money out of the attic window – now a prosperous man of business, with a beautiful home of his own, and himself a leading member in a thriving church.

One of Moody's strong points was his ability to keep everyone around him hard at work. His method may be described in a single word – leadership. He was not skillful in giving minute directions, but he was always ahead, and they learned to follow him, and to do as he did. He was as ready to go down, as to go up, to find and save a sinner; indeed, he was always ready to go anywhere or do anything which gave promise of such a result. It was impossible to be with him and not feel the contagion of his energy and faith. Scholars as well as teachers caught it from him, and began to be missionaries on their own account, searching out and bringing in new scholars and keeping the enthusiasm of the school always at fever heat.

Prizes were sometimes offered for the largest number of new scholars brought in. On one occasion he presented the most successful young missionary with a pet lamb, a somewhat unusual gift of a Sunday school, but one which served as a striking and valuable object lesson, which Moody was not slow to use.

Among the band of young converts, which all the time increased around him, was a girl whose father owned a small vessel with which he freighted lumber. Having given her own heart to the Savior, she tried to persuade her father to do the same. But he was a man having no taste for religion, though he was very fond of the child. He took her with him on a certain voyage, during which she tried in vain to establish a prayer meeting in the little cabin and to convert some of the crew. On arriving at the lumber camp, this little missionary commenced a Sunday school, as nearly as possible like the North Market Mission. Not content with this, and hearing of another encampment of woodcutters similar to their own, she opened a second school among them also. During the severe northern winter, she presided personally over both these institutions; riding on horseback through the woods every Sabbath, after the manner of the early Methodist pioneers.

It may be supposed that these two schools in the woods were of a very simple character, since the little girl herself was the entire force of officers and teachers; and all the library and literature in use among them was her own little copy of the New Testament. The results of her labor cannot now be given; but it is easy to imagine the tender interest with which those rough woodsmen sat at the feet of their child-missionary, charmed by her Christian courage, and cheered by her simple faith.

The lumber season being over, the little vessel started for Chicago. During the voyage, a terrible storm arose, disabling the craft and driving it rapidly toward a lee shore. The crew being completely exhausted, and expecting in a few minutes to be drowned, begged the little girl to pray for them, which she did with the greatest composure. When she had told the good Lord all about them, and asked Him to take them out of their danger, if He thought best, and, above all things, to forgive their sins and make them ready for heaven, she began, in a clear, sweet voice, to sing that little Sunday school hymn,

"We are joyously voyaging over the main,
Bound for the evergreen shore."

With the song, new strength and hope seemed to come to the arms and hearts of the crew; and renewing their efforts to weather the point which threatened their destruction, and aided, perhaps, by some slight change in the wind or abatement of the storm, the little craft weathered the rocks of the headland close enough to toss a biscuit ashore, and then swung out safely on the open course for home.

To keep such assembly in order was of course impossible; though a degree of confusion which would have been fatal to an ordinary Sunday school was no serious objection here. But sometimes a wild young barbarian would make his appearance, defying all authority to disturb the meeting.

There was one big fellow in particular who insisted on bringing his street manners into the schoolroom. All kinds of moral suasion seemed to be wasted on him. He was too big to be frightened, and too ignorant to be ashamed. After bearing with him for a long time, during which he continued to grow worse instead of better, Moody and his friends began to fear that they had at last found one boy for whom nothing could be done. A great many evil spirits had been cast out by the influence of that school, but this one seemed determined to stay. To turn a scholar away as hopelessly bad would be a disgraceful confession of failure; besides, it was contrary to all their ideas of the Gospel to shut this young ruffian out from the means of grace, when he was in such evident need of them.

A solemn council was held one Sunday, but no one could think of any new method of reaching this desperate case. All the week it lay heavy on Moody's mind. The next Sabbath the big fellow appeared, more uproarious than ever; there was actual danger of his breaking up the school.

On this memorable day Mr. Moody determined to try the last remedy. His ample physical endowment for missionary work has already been mentioned, of which on this day he made a very effective use. Coming suddenly upon the fellow, in the middle of the crowded hall, he seized him with both hands, fairly lifted him off his legs, carried him into a little ante-room, locked the door, and proceeded to apply the treatment recommended by Solomon. This was by no means an easy task, for the culprit was as strong and active and savage as a wolf. The noise of the struggle awakened the most lively interest of the school, and by way of diversion Mr. Farwell started a song. Thus on the two sides of that bolted door two widely different means of grace were in simultaneous operation.

In due course of time Moody and his pupil emerged from the ante-room, both greatly flushed, and one completely subdued.

"It was hard work," said Moody; "but I think we have saved him."

Mr. Farwell met this very boy, now grown to a man, at the noon prayer-meeting. They recognized each other, and heartily agreed that Moody was right in applying desperate remedies for desperate diseases.

After that, his school was no more disturbed by such ruffians.

He had shown a new claim to their admiration and respect. Order thus enforced became sacred in the opinion of all.

A lad – the one nicknamed "Indian" – coming into the school one day, found a raw recruit sitting with his cap on. Instantly he drew it off, and hit the offender a blow between the eyes which laid him sprawling on the floor. "I'll learn you better than to wear your hat in this school," said he; and then he passed quietly to his place, feeling the high satisfaction of having done his duty.

One of Moody's friends reported a family to him where there were several children who were due at the North Market School, but whose father was a notorious, infidel rum-seller, and would not let them come.

The missionary at once called upon him; but as soon as he made known his errand he was obliged to "get out of that place" very quickly, in order to save his head. Again and again he called, only to be driven away with curses and blasphemies. "I would rather my son should be a thief, and my daughter a harlot, than have you make fools and Christians of them over there at your Sunday school," said the desperate man. But still Moody would not give up the case.

One day, finding the man in a little better humor than usual, he asked him if he had ever read the New Testament, to which the publican replied that he had not, and on his part inquired if Moody had ever read Paine's "Age of Reason." Finding he had never done so, the man proposed to read the Testament if he would read the "Age of Reason." To this Moody at once agreed.

"He had the best of the bargain; but it gave me a chance to call again to bring him the book," said Moody.

After wading through that mass of infidel abominations, he called on the publican again to see how he got on with the Testament; but found him full of objections and hot for debate.

"See here, young man," said he; "you are inviting me and

my family to go to meeting; now you may have a meeting here if you like."

"What! will you let me preach here in your saloon?"

"Yes."

"And will you bring in your family, and let me bring in the neighbors?"

"Yes. But mind, you are not to do all the talking. I and my friends will have something to say."

"All right. You shall have forty-five minutes, and I will have fifteen."

The time for the meeting was set, but when Moody reached the place he found that the company had removed to a larger house in the neighborhood, where a crowd of atheists, blasphemers, and wild characters in great variety were waiting for a chance to make mincemeat of the young missionary and use up the New Testament forever.

"You shall begin," said Moody.

Upon this they began to ask him questions.

"No questions" said he. "I haven't come to argue with you, but to preach Christ to you. Go on and say what you like, and then I will speak."

Then they began to talk among themselves; but it was not long before they quarreled over their own different unbeliefs, so that what began as a debate was in danger of ending in a fight.

"Order! Your time is up," said Moody. "I am in the habit of beginning my addresses with prayer. Let us pray."

"Stop! stop!" said one. "There's no use in your praying. Besides, your Bible says there must be 'two agreed' if there is to be any praying; and you are all alone."

Without attempting to correct this false quotation, Moody replied that perhaps some of them might feel like praying before he got through; and so, he opened his heart to God.

When he had finished, a little boy who had been converted

in the Mission School and had come with his friend to this strange meeting, began to pray. His childish voice and simple faith at once attracted the closest attention. As he went on telling the Lord all about those wicked men and begging Him to help them to believe in Jesus Christ, the Holy Ghost fell upon the assembly. A great solemnity came over those hardhearted infidels and scoffers; there was not a dry eye in the room. Pretty soon they began to be frightened. They rushed out, some by one door and some by the other – did not stop to hear a word of the sermon, but fled from the place as if it had been haunted.

As a result of this meeting, Moody captured all the old infidel's children for his Sunday school; and, a little while after, the man himself stood up in the noonday prayer-meeting and begged them to pray for his miserable soul.

Striking out in all directions, taking no thought of the prejudices or passions of those he met, but urging them all to come at once to Christ, and to the North Market Mission, it was impossible but that he should make a good many enemies. One old woman, whose children he was inviting to his Sunday school, seized a butcher's knife and rushed out to kill him. But he easily got away.

Three ruffians, who had threatened him with a beating, came into his prayer-room one night just after the meeting was over, when there was no one present but himself and a lad. Knowing their errand, he invited them to sit down till he had gathered up his hymnbooks and Testaments, at the same time motioning the lad to leave.

Unlike his first place of meeting, this room was lighted with gas, a single jet of which was burning. Towards this he made his way, picking up his books as he went along; and then, as quick as a flash, he turned out the light, sprang over the benches in the darkness, and was off before his enemies suspected his design.

Such slight annoyances as these, however, soon ceased to

disturb his mind. He became accustomed to them. But what did really worry him was the boys disturbing his meetings and breaking the windows of the place in which they were held.

When the strain on his patience came to be too severe, Moody determined to strike at the root of the matter; and accordingly went to Bishop Duggan, the Romish prelate of Chicago, and laid his grievance before him. He told the bishop that he was trying to do good, in a part of the city which everybody else had neglected; and that it was a shame that the members of the bishop's church should break the windows of his schoolroom.

The zeal and boldness of the man surprised and delighted the bishop; who promised that the lambs of his flock should hereafter be duly restrained. Moody, thus encouraged, went on to say that he often came upon sick people who were Roman Catholics; he should be very glad to pray with them and relieve them, but they were so suspicious of him that they would not allow him to come near them. Now, if the bishop would give him a good word to those people, it would help him amazingly in his work of charity.

Such a request from a heretical Protestant was probably never made of a Catholic bishop before. But he very kindly replied that he should be most happy to give the recommendation if Mr. Moody would only join the Catholic Church; telling him at the same time he seemed to be too good and valuable a man to be a heretic.

"I am afraid that would hinder me in my work among the Protestants," said Moody.

"Not at all," answered the bishop.

"What! do you mean to say that I could go to the noon prayer-meeting, and pray with all kinds of Christian people – Baptists, Methodists, Presbyterians, all together – just as I do now?"

"Oh yes," replied the bishop; "if it were necessary, you might do that."

"So, then, Protestants and Catholics can pray together, can they?"

"Yes."

"Well, bishop, this is a very important matter, and ought to be attended to at once. No man wants to belong to the true Church more than I do. I wish you would pray for me right here, that God would show me His true Church, and help me to be a worthy member of it."

Of course, the prelate could not refuse; so they knelt down together; and the bishop prayed very lovingly for the heretic, and when he had finished, the heretic began to pray for the bishop.

From that day to the day of his death, Bishop Duggan and Mr. Moody were good friends. The bishop made no progress in converting him, it is true; but he stopped his wild young parishioners from breaking the prayer room windows; and if only Moody would have joined the Church of Rome there is no telling to what high dignities he might have come!

This incident was published recently in London, and a Catholic priest who read it called on Mr. Moody, and actually labored with him for a long time, with the utmost zeal and earnestness, in the hope that he might be persuaded into the Church of Peter and Mary.

"If you would only join the true Church," said the priest, "you would be the greatest man in England."

But, as may easily be supposed, this kind of argument made no impression upon a man who is more honored in bringing thousands of lost sinners to Christ than he would be by a seat in the chair of St. Peter himself.

Mr. Moody had frequently been asked how he came to give up mercantile life, in which his prospect for success were so promising. He invariably made this reply: "The way God led me out of business into Christian work was as follows:

"I had never lost sight of Jesus Christ since the first night

I met him in the store at Boston. But for years I was only a nominal Christian, really believing that I could not work for God. No one had ever asked me to do anything.

"When I went to Chicago, I hired five pews in a church, and used to go out on the street and pick up young men and fill these pews. I never spoke to those young men about their souls; that was the work of the elders, I thought.

"After working for some time like that, I started a mission Sabbath school. I thought numbers were everything, and so I worked for numbers. When the attendance ran below 1,000 it troubled me; and when it ran to 1,200 or 1,500 I was elated. Still none was converted; there was no harvest.

"Then God opened my eyes. There was a class of young ladies in the school, who were without exception the most frivolous set of girls I ever met. One Sunday the teacher was ill and I took that class. They laughed in my face, and I felt like opening the door and telling them all to get out and never come back.

"That week the teacher of the class came into the store where I worked. He was pale and looked very ill.

"'What is the trouble?' I asked.

"'I have had another hemorrhage of my lungs. The doctor says I cannot live on Lake Michigan, so I am going to New York State. I suppose I am going home to die.' He seemed greatly troubled, and when I asked him the reason he replied: 'Well, I have never led any of my class to Christ. I really believe I have done the girls more harm than good.'

"I had never heard anyone talk like that before, and it set me thinking. After a while I said: 'Suppose you go and tell them how you feel. I will go with you in a carriage, if you want to go.' He consented, and we started out together. It was one of the best journeys I ever had on earth. We went to the house of one of the girls, called for her, and the teacher talked to her about her soul. There was no laughing then! Tears stood in her eyes before long. After he had explained the way of life he suggested that we have prayer. He asked me to pray. True, I had never done such a thing in my life as to pray God to convert a young lady there and then. But we prayed, and God answered our prayer.

"We went to other houses. He would go upstairs and be all out of breath, and he would tell the girls what he had come for. It wasn't long before they broke down and sought salvation. When his strength gave out, I took him back to his lodgings. The next day we went out again. At the end of ten days, he came to the store with his face literally shining.

"'Mr. Moody,' he said, 'the last one of my class has yielded herself to Christ.' I tell you we had a time of rejoicing. He had to leave the next night, so I called his class together that night for a prayer meeting, and there God kindled a fire in my soul that has never gone out. The height of my ambition had been to be a successful merchant, and if I had known that meeting was going to take that ambition out of me I might not have gone. But how many times I have thanked God since for that meeting!

"The dying teacher sat in the midst of his class and talked with them and read the fourteenth chapter of John. We tried to sing "Blest be the tie that binds," after which we knelt down to prayer. I was just rising from my knees when one of the class began to pray for her dying teacher. Another prayed, and another, and before we rose the whole class had prayed. As I went out I said to myself: 'Oh God, let me die rather than lose the blessing I have received tonight.'

"The next evening, I went to the depot to say good-bye to that teacher. Just before the train started one of the class came, and before long, without any prearrangement, they were all there. What a meeting that was! We tried to sing, but we broke down. The last we saw of that dying teacher he was standing on the platform of the car, his finger pointing upward, telling that class to meet him in heaven.

"I didn't know what this was going to cost me. I was disqualified for business; it had become distasteful to me. I had got a taste of another world and cared no more for making money. For some days after the greatest struggle of my life took place. Should I give up business and give myself to Christian work or should I not? I have never regretted my choice. Oh, the luxury of leading some one out of the darkness of this world into the glorious light and liberty of the gospel."

Mr. Moody and the Young Men's Christian Association – Camp and Field

The great revival of 1857-58 led to organizing the Young Men's Christian Association of Chicago.

Its first important work was the establishment of a daily noon prayer-meeting, which, during the winter and spring, was very well attended. But after a while the impetus was lost, and the meetings grew smaller and smaller, until at last they seemed likely to die. From the first, Moody had made himself conspicuous in these meetings by his blunt manners and bold attacks upon fashionable sins, such as tippling, the use of tobacco, going to the theatre, playing billiards, and other loaferish games. He was very severe against professors of religion who wish to enjoy as many pleasures of sin as possible, without spoiling their hopes of heaven – Christians who are so nearly like the people of the world that, except on Sunday, it is very hard to tell the difference.

On this account he came to be looked upon with disfavor. Many sensitive people left off attending the noon prayer-meeting for fear of this bold brother, in whose eyes sin was sin wherever it might be found, and who was so insensible to the dignities of wealth, fashion, station, and age, that no offender was safe from being held up on the point of his spear.

But Moody, having once put his hand to the plough, he never

looked back. Therefore the coldness of some of his brethren produced no discouragement in his mind. A man who had achieved such success in the North Market Mission, which had been started against the advice of every clergyman in the neighborhood, was not likely to be troubled by criticisms.

The waning interest in the noon prayer-meeting roused him to new efforts on its behalf. When the attendance fell to half a dozen, he was one of the six; and when there were but three he was one of the three.

One day, all brethren being out of town, nobody went to the prayer-meeting but one old Scotch woman. This excellent person set great store by the noon meeting, and, when no one else appeared, she determined to hold it herself rather than have it fail even for a single day. So, after waiting a long time, she put on her spectacles, went forward to the leader's desk, read a passage of Scripture, talked it over to herself, for the comfort of her old heart, and then offered prayer for the languishing meeting, and for the outpouring of the Holy Spirit upon it, and upon the city. Prayer being ended, she sung a psalm, and, the time having thus been all improved, she went comfortably home, feeling that she had done her duty, gained a blessing, and saved the noon prayer-meeting from utter extinction.

On relating her solitary experience, some of the brethren were deeply impressed by it. Mr. Moody at once set about the business of bringing in recruits; and so well did he succeed that very soon there was a large and regular attendance, and the meeting began to be marked with the presence of the Spirit of the Lord.

Recognizing his pre-eminent ability, the Young Men's Christian Association had appointed him Chairman of the Visiting Committee to the sick and to strangers. In the duties of this office he scoured the city in all directions; and very soon Moody and his pony became a familiar sight, especially in the regions of The Sands, the Association Rooms, and the North Market Hall. An old resident on the North Side, who was familiar with him in those days, declares that he would chase the wild small-fry up the streets and down the alleys, and, after a Sunday morning's search for new scholars, would emerge from some dirty lane, or court, his pony literally covered with ragged urchins, followed by others of the same sort, holding on by the tail, caching by the stirrups, or clinging to each other's rags; and these he would march in grand procession down the North Market Sunday School.

The increasing attendance at the noon prayer-meeting had occasioned its removal to a large back room in the Methodist Church block. To this place Moody removed his residence, that is, removed himself. Having no longer any money, he determined fully to test the question whether God would really take care of him in his new work. At length he was brought to the necessity of sleeping on the benches of the prayer-room and living on crackers and cheese. But he kept on with his work all the same. He collected considerable sums of money for the poor, and for the various works of charity and religion carried on by the Association; but he would not use a penny of it for himself, because it was not given for that specific purpose.

Presently, without a word from him, some of his friends began to wonder how he was living; and, finding out the poverty of his bed and board, they insisted on supplying him with abundant comforts of life.

His zeal and devotion were the life and hope of the Association; but he shocked the nice sense of propriety of some of these gentlemen by carrying its work among a class of people who had hitherto been neglected, under the impression that its proper line of effort was among the higher classes of young men.

Under Moody's leadership, the Young Men's Christian Association became, like the North Market Mission, a free and popular institution, extending its influence to all classes of society, and bringing the cultured and wealthy to the assistance of the ignorant and the poor.

At the breaking out of the war, in 1861, the devotional committee of the Young Men's Christian Association, of which Mr. Moody was chairman, found a new line of work made ready to their hands. On the arrival of the first regiment, ordered to Camp Douglas for instruction, the committee was on the ground, and before the tents were fairly pitched, a camp prayer-meeting was in progress.

It was a matter of no little surprise and joy to the soldiers, many of whom had come from churches, Sunday schools, and Christian homes, to hear themselves saluted in the name of Christ almost before they could stack their arms, and to have the very first tent which was pitched in their camp put to its first use as a place for prayer. Christian zeal kept pace with patriotism. Mr. Moody and his committee were obliged to call for help; a hundred and fifty clergymen and laymen promptly responded to the call. Every evening eight or ten meetings were held in different camps; and an almost continued service, within reach of every regiment, on the Sabbath. Over fifteen hundred of these services were held in and around Chicago by the Association during the war.

In these meetings, Mr. Moody seemed almost ubiquitous; he would hasten from one barrack and camp to another, day and night, week-days and Sundays, praying, exhorting, conversing personally with the men about their souls, and reveling in the abundant work and swift success which the war had brought within his reach.

The chapel of the Young Men's Christian Association at Camp Douglas was the first camp chapel in existence – being built in the October of 1861.

Meanwhile, many of the soldier converts had been sent to

the field, and, feeling the want of the means of grace which they had left behind, they sent repeated calls to the Chicago brethren to come down and establish similar meetings among them. In response to this invitation Mr. Moody was sent to the army near Fort Donelson – being the first regular army delegate from Chicago. Similar labors by other Associations led to a convention in Norfolk, Virginia, on the 16th of November, 1861, where the United States Christian Commission was projected.

The news of the battle of Fort Donelson, on the 15th of February, 1862, was the signal for sending to the field a special committee of relief, composed of the Rev. Robert Patterson, D. D., Mr. Moody, and Mr. Jacobs. With them went a number of other brethren from Chicago, eager to minister to the sick and wounded and dying.

Like the men who go down to the sea in ships, Moody and his brethren saw God's wonders in camp and field. Having so many sinners to point to the Savior, and so little time in which to do it, they prayed to the Lord to do His "short work." So many men found the Savior, and died while they were praying for them, that they came to have a strange familiarity with heaven. These souls seemed to be messengers between them and God, carrying up continually the fresh and glowing record of the work they were doing in His name. And so simple and easy did it become for them to "ask and receive," that they were rather surprised if the penitent for whose conversion they prayed was not blessed before they reached the Amen.

These wonders of grace in camp and field were reported at the Chicago noon prayer-meeting by Mr. Moody and his co-laborers, on their return from their frequent excursions to the front. By this means a very intimate connection was kept up between the work in the army and the work at home, and the meeting became intensely interesting – especially to those whose husbands, sons, and brothers, were fighting for the Union.

Strangely enough, as though no other place were so near to heaven, and no other believers had such access to the ear of the Lord, people from all over the State, and even from neighboring States, used to send requests for prayer to be read at the Chicago noon prayer meeting. These requests were received by thousands; and often, in quick succession, came the tidings of glorious answers to prayer, with offerings of glad thanksgiving, and sometimes gifts of money and supplies for helping on the work of the Commission.

One of the marvels of those days was the revival of religion among the rebel prisoners, about ten thousand of whom had been taken at Fort Donelson and brought to Camp Douglass, which was transformed from a camp of instruction into a prison. Mr. Moody was impressed with the thought that these poor men needed the means of grace fully as much as the Union soldiers; but to gain access to them was a matter of extreme difficulty. One day he succeeded in obtaining a permit to visit them, which he gave to his friend Mr. Hawley, the Young Men's Christian Associations Secretary; and himself took a can of kerosene oil to light up with, it being towards evening, hoping, in the capacity of a servant, to be allowed to pass the guard along with his more clerical-looking friend. But it was of no use; the guard would not let in two men on one permit, though Mr. Moody exhibited his can of oil, and declared he was only going with the other gentleman to help along the meeting.

The earnest discussion was overheard by the officer of the day, who came up to see what the matter was; and recognizing Mr. Moody, he took him to headquarters, vouched for his being all right, and obtained a pass for him to go in and hold meetings with the prisoners as often as he liked. In a few minutes he rejoined his friend Hawley in the prison. They announced the purpose of their visit; and the men, being both surprised and pleased, gathered around them while they read the Scriptures, exhorted, and prayed.

At the very first meeting, the power of God was manifest, and a large number of the prisoners were inquiring what they must do to be saved. Meetings were held with them every afternoon and evening. The flame of revival spread throughout their entire camp. The tidings flew over the whole city and county, and produced the most intense excitement. Great numbers of clergymen and lay workers begged for the privilege of assisting in the meetings. It was held to be a peculiar honor to lead one of those enemies to Christ. Great numbers were soundly converted; and, returned to their Southern homes thanking God for their bonds, in which His servants had found them out, and where they, though prisoners of war, had found peace and liberty in the Savior.

In all this work Mr. Moody bore an important and honorable part. His frequent excursions to battlefields and camps made him, more than any other man, the medium of communication between the work in the army and the work at home. He was on the field after the battles of Pittsburgh Landing, Shiloh, and Murfreesboro, with the army at Chattanooga, and was one of the first to enter Richmond, where he ministered alike to friend and foe.

After the war, Mr. Moody renewed his labors in Chicago with redoubled vigor. The north side mission had grown in numbers and influence. He decided that a tabernacle was necessary and that $20,000 would be required. The building was erected in Illinois street. He consulted with other ministers and it was decided to organize a church. This was the beginning of the famous "Chicago Avenue church," the present building being put up after the destruction of the original tabernacle by the great fire. The new church began with a membership of 300.

In 1864, Mr. Moody was married to Miss Emma C. Revell.

Three children were born to them – Emma, William, and Paul. Mr. Moody's aged mother died in 1896 and until her death lived in Northfield, adjoining the great evangelist's home.

The great fire in 1871 changed the whole current of Mr. Moody's life work, but not at once. With his wife and two children, he was roused in the middle of the night to find the fierce fire approaching their dwelling, and, leaving his little store of worldly goods to their fate, he had to seek shelter in the house of a friend. Mr. Moody's school and church were swept away, but in one month after the fire, a temporary erection was completed and services again held.

Besides caring for his own school and church Mr. Moody sent out an appeal as president for the Young Men's Christian Association, for help to rebuild. Money flowed in from Great Britain and elsewhere. When the Association building was well under way, Mr. Moody began to think of permanent premises for his school and church. When the building fund was started, money came from all parts. Among the unique gifts was a colossal subscription from 500,000 Sunday school children of 5 cents each, all anxious to have a brick in Mr. Moody's tabernacle. From Pekin, China, he received $300 from converted Chinamen. A start was made at building the new church, but for some time only the basement story was used and it was not until years afterward that the present handsome structure was completed and occupied.

Moody and Sankey Meet – Evangelist Induces the Noted Singer to Join Him

It was the hiatus following the shock of the great fire that turned Mr. Moody toward a much-broader, international evangelistic work. He was very active in the national work of the Young Men's Christian Association convention in Indianapolis. It was here that he met Ira D. Sankey, who later became his singing partner in revival work on two continents. It is said that Moody was dragging a prayer meeting along under the deadening influence of one who was attempting to lead the singing. Sankey came in and was recognized by one who knew his musical ability. He was asked to handle the music and soon put life into the meeting.

"Where do you live?" asked Moody of Sankey at the close of the meeting.

"In Newcastle, Pa," replied Sankey.

"I want you," said Moody with no explanation.

"What for?"

"To help me in my work in Chicago.".

"I can't leave my business," said Sankey.

"You must. I have been looking for you for eight years. You must give up your business and come to Chicago with me."

Sankey came and for years the two evangelists worked together in Chicago. The new style of revival music shocked some of the ministers, but it won popular favor.

In 1872 Moody and Sankey sailed for Liverpool, England, on direct invitation of English friends. Not having had a house of his own since the fire, Mr. Moody took his wife and children along. On arriving in England, they began their labor in York, on the east coast. Progress was slow, but by degrees they won the confidence of the people. They visited Sunderland, Newcastle, and Carlisle in the north of England and interest in their services began to grow. Newcastle especially responded with many converts. Some Scotch friends, hearing of the revival, invited Moody and Sankey to pay a visit to Edinburgh. They went thither and began a series of services that shook orthodox Scotland to its foundations. It was the spark to the dry tinder of centuries of formalism, and preachers and congregations alike were affected. Converts were made by thousands and there were no halls in the Scotch cities large enough to contain the audience that thronged to hear the Americans.

For the next three years Moody and Sankey held revival services in all parts of Great Britain, concluding in 1875 with the remarkable thirty days' meeting in London. Professor Drummond, the Scotch writer, has said that Scotland would not be what it is today had it missed the year of Moody and Sankey. There are today in all parts of the United Kingdom buildings and institutions bearing the names of Moody and Sankey. A writer in the Edinburgh Review compared the visit of Moody and Sankey to Scotland with the reformation of Martin Luther in its moral power and with the evangelism of Whitfield and Wesley in its sweeping results.

All the larger centers of population in Scotland, Ireland, and England were the scene of a remarkable religious awakening during the visits of Moody and Sankey.

When the evangelists sailed from Liverpool on their return to America there was an enormous crowd of people to bid them bon voyage. They were the recipients of thousands of messages of good will and earnest invitations to pay a second visit. On arrival in the United States the two evangelists plunged at once into a series of meetings in all the larger cities. Their work was in some degree a repetition of the success in Great Britain as to crowds and converts.

Mr. Moody at Northfield

Northfield is today the physical evidence of Moody's greatness as an educator as well as an evangelist. When in 1875 Moody, accompanied by Mr. Sankey, returned to America after an epoch-making tour of revivalism in Great Britain, it was expected that the evangelist would select Chicago for his home, as it had formerly been. But Moody had larger plans, and recognized that for the rest of his life he was to be a world evangelist without an abiding city. He would have to retire occasionally for a brief respite from his public labors and provide a shelter for his family. It was this twin purpose, as described by Mr. Moody himself, that first turned his thoughts to Northfield, his birthplace, as a permanent home. Nowhere could a more restful spot have been found. The trees, which line the long, wide avenue in double rows on each side, are tall and of vast girth and in the hottest days create ample shade. The old-fashioned white houses stand some distance from the road and from each other, and are mostly surrounded with lawns and flower beds. The old homestead which was Mr. Moody's birthplace was occupied by his mother until her death. It is a plain, old farmhouse, fronting upon a country road which branches from the main street of the village and winds easterly up the hillside toward a mountain district. It looks out upon orchards and meadows and has a large tree in its front dooryard.

When Mr. Moody decided to make a permanent home in Northfield, he bought for about $3,000 a plain but roomy frame house, with grounds, at the north end of the town near his mother's house. The building fronts on the main road. To the building as Mr. Moody found it he made additions from time to time as they were required. His study was on the first floor near the entrance. Here was his working library. A fine clock, much admired by visitors, was sent to him by a lady in England who had been helped in the Christian life by Moody's illustration of a pendulum. Everything about the house was characterized by simplicity and the best conditions of effective work. In the heart of Northfield, Rev. Dr. Pentecost of Brooklyn also purchased a commodious residence, and still further south is a modest white cottage which Mr. Sankey also bought and fitted up as a summer home, to be near his fellow evangelist.

Mr. Moody was no sooner domiciled in Northfield than he began to turn his attention to remedying the lack of educational facilities for the young people of the neighborhood. He was still a tremendous worker in the outside evangelistic field, but whenever he returned to Northfield the desire to benefit the young with schooling facilities was uppermost. His own early education had been deficient, and it became a fixed purpose of his life to remove a similar deficiency for the new generation of young people growing up in Northfield and vicinity. He first planned a school for girls. He built a small addition to his own house, with room for eight girls, and when twenty girls had been admitted to these cramped quarters, with others seeking entrance, he built a small brick dormitory and classroom on the other side of the street. This was also soon over-crowded, and Mr. Moody, with the help of a retired Boston merchant, bought a hillside farm adjoining his own and his mother's holdings to the north. Plans for a building were begun and in 1879 the handsome brick building now known as East hall was erected.

Its situation is more commanding than any of the other buildings put up later. It affords a superb view to the west and north. The foreground is the eastern slope of the Connecticut valley and the river can be seen at intervals throughout many miles of its winding course. The western slope of the valley, partly wooded, culminates in a range of forest-clad hills. In the direction of Vermont is a wide landscape, fading into distant mountain peaks. East hall cost about $30,000, was designed as a dormitory, and accommodates sixty students. The small brick building near Mr. Moody's house was for some time used in connection with it as a recitation hall. An additional dormitory was remodeled out of a large dwelling house farther north and named Bonar hall, after Rev. Dr. Bonar of Glasgow. This latter building was destroyed by fire in March, 1886.

From the first Mr. Moody had kept down the charge of board and tuition for his girls to $100 a year. The expense for each student was about $160 a year, the balance being made up by benevolent contributions. Applications increased at such rate that it was decided in 1881 to build another large dormitory.

Moody was himself absent in England during most of the next three years, but during his absence American friends and coworkers put up a large brick dormitory, costing about $60,000. The building was finished in 1884 and was named Marquand hall. Its site is to the northwest of East hall. The building is used entirely as a dormitory and accommodates about eighty students. About midway between Marquand hall and East hall a handsome building of brick and granite, called Recitation hall, was completed in 1885. The cost of the latter building, like a similar one afterward put up at Mount Hermon, was borne by the hymn-book fund. Moody used to say when pointing to either structure: "Mr. Sankey sang that building up."

In fitting up the Recitation hall it was arranged that partitions could be removed and the whole thrown into one auditorium. This hall has been the scene of many of the most memorable gatherings in Northfield of later years. In the same building are chemical, physical, and botanical laboratories. A library building has also been given by generous friends. Improvements have been made on the grounds, which now have a parklike aspect. Winding drives connect the buildings with the main thoroughfare. The seminary grounds include more than 250 acres. There is an artificial lake, whose cost was borne by John Wanamaker of Philadelphia. Many additions and improvements have been made within recent years, but the seminary rules are the same as at the institution's humble beginning.[1] Instead of scores the pupils are now numbered by hundreds. The curriculum is as thorough as in most girls' schools, with the addition of specific Christian training. A graduate of Wellesley college, Miss Evelyn S. Hall, organized the original teaching staff, which is still noted for proficiency.

While the Northfield seminary was still in its infant state Mr. Moody decided to have also a school for boys.

---

[1] As of this writing in the early 1900's. This is hardly likely to be the case today.

His first purchase for this end was a 400-acre farm in the town of Gill, about four miles from Northfield, in a southwesterly direction, across the Connecticut. He bought 200 acres first for $7,000 and a little later the other 200 acres for $5,500. The Connecticut River railroad traverses the site. The height upon which Mr. Moody decided to build his boys' school is now called Mount Hermon. There is a picturesque drive from Northfield to Mount Hermon. The river is crossed by a wire-rope ferry and there is telephone communication between the buildings of both institutions. The money with which the Mount Hermon property was bought was the gift of Hiram Camp, who wrote his check for $25,000.

At first the old farmhouses found upon the place were used as dormitories. A small wooden building was first put up to serve as a recitation hall. When more dormitory room was needed, Mr. Moody concluded to try the family system. Instead of housing a large number of boys in one building, they were divided into groups of not more than twenty and housed in small cottages, each under the charge of two matrons. In 1885 a large building of brick and granite, called Recitation hall, was completed and dedicated. It contains class and recitation rooms, library, chapel, and museum. There is a splendid view from the cupola of this building. After a few years Mr. Moody changed his plans and raised the age of admission for boys to 16 years and enlarged the course of study. This broke up the family system to some extent, and new buildings on a large scale were begun in 1885. In June, 1886, a large dormitory, called Crossley hall, was dedicated. Later a large, brick dining hall was erected, and within recent years there have been many additions, making the Mount Hermon seminary one of the best equipped boys' schools in the east.

Mr. Moody always had strong views as to the admission and training of his scholars of both sexes. At Mount Hermon the cost of board and tuition was also placed at $100 a year, so that none was barred on the ground of expense. At Mount Hermon the students have always been required to perform a certain amount of manual labor in addition to class work. Some are employed on the farm, some in the laundry and some in housework. The students are for the most part a picked body of young, vigorous Christians, who have been drawn to Mr. Moody's school from all parts of the earth. There are students from Germany, Scandinavia, Turkey, and even American Indians and Japanese. Of course, the main body of students is of American extraction, and a large proportion of them are in training for missionary work. Whenever he was at Northfield, Mr. Moody gave regular courses of lectures at both of his schools, and distinguished educators from all other seats of learning have been frequent lecturers.

Besides his schools, Northfield, under Mr. Moody's direction, became the center of gatherings of religious workers, culminating in the famous summer conventions which were begun in 1880. For nine months of every year up to the last year of his life, Mr. Moody was engrossed in arduous evangelistic labor in various parts of the country. His idea of a vacation was to throw himself into his Northfield educational work and to plan big conventions which made Northfield a summer city. He called his first convention of Christian workers in 1880. The only large building then constructed was the one now known as East hall, behind which a capacious camp was pitched. Under this canopy from day to day were held meetings whose influence was world-wide.

In 1881 a convention was called for bible study and continued for thirty days. Rev. Dr. Bonar of Glasgow, who had just served as moderator of the general assembly of the Free Church of Scotland, was a principal figure at this gathering. Dozens of equally prominent clergymen and evangelists attended, and Mr.

Sankey conducted the singing. For the next three years, owing to Mr. Moody's absence in England, there were no conventions, but in 1885 there was another August convention. Every year since they have grown in interest. The attendance has averaged from 300 to 500 from a distance, and with the people of the vicinity the meeting often averaged 1,500. Moody was always the life and soul of these conventions, and of late years many of the most prominent regular pastors in England and America have taken part.

Special conventions of college students have also been held under Mr. Moody's personal leadership. Whether the great evangelist's death will lessen the fame of Northfield as a convention city is a melancholy problem for a host of his friends and co-workers.

Mr. Moody was stricken with heart trouble in Kansas City on Nov. 16, 1899, while holding revival meetings at the Convention hall. He was compelled to give up his work, and on the day following, started east in the care of a physician.

Mr. Moody addressed great crowds during his stay at Kansas City. The meetings began on Sunday, Nov. 12. The crowds were immense, thousands of people filling the hall afternoon and evening each day. The strain on Mr. Moody was great. He preached his last sermon on Thursday night, Nov. 16, fully 15,000 people listening to an earnest appeal which many stamped as one of the evangelist's greatest efforts. He was stricken the next morning at his hotel, but laughingly declared he was all right, and that he would be able to preach that afternoon.

After he reached Northfield eminent physicians were consulted and everything was done to prolong life.

Conscious up to the moment his eyes closed, well knowing his last sleep was about to begin, he died at 11:50 o'clock, Dec. 22, 1899. The end came quietly, peacefully, at his home in this village, which he loved so well and near to the scenes of many of his triumphs.

Mr. Moody first knew that the end was very near at 8 o'clock the previous night. He was satisfied that he would not recover, and when the doctor confirmed his opinion he said:

"The world is receding and heaven opening."

During the night Mr. Moody had a number of sinking spells. Despite his suffering he was kindness itself to those about him.

At 7:30 o'clock in the morning Dr. Wood was again called. When he reached Mr. Moody's room he found his patient in a semi-conscious condition. When Mr. Moody recovered consciousness he said, with all his old vivacity:

"What's the matter; what's going on here?"

"Father, you haven't been quite so well, and so we came in to see you," a member of the family replied. A little later Mr. Moody said to his sons:

"I have always been an ambitious man – not ambitious to lay up wealth, but to find work to do."

Mr. Moody urged his two boys and Mr. Fitt to see that the schools at Northfield, at Mount Herman, and the Chicago Bible Institute should receive their best care. This they assured Mr. Moody they would do.

During the forenoon Mrs. Fitt, his daughter, said to him: "Father, we can't spare you." Mr. Moody's reply was:

"I'm not going to throw my life away. If God has more work for me to do I'll not die."

He was thoroughly conscious until within less than a minute of his death and told his family that as God called, he was ready to go. At one time he told the attending physician not to give him any more medicine to revive him, as calling him back simply prolonged the agony for his family. In his closing hours there was no note of sadness, but one of triumph.

Similar Updated Classics

The Way to God, by Dwight L. Moody

There is life in Christ. Rich, joyous, wonderful life. It is true that the Lord disciplines those whom He loves and that we are often tempted by the world and our enemy, the devil. But if we know how to go beyond that temptation to cling to the cross of Jesus Christ and keep our eyes on our Lord, our reward both here on earth and in heaven will be 100 times better than what this world has to offer.

This book is thorough. It brings to life the love of God, examines the state of the unsaved individual's soul, and analyzes what took place on the cross for our sins. *The Way to God* takes an honest look at our need to repent and follow Jesus, and gives hope for unending, joyous eternity in heaven.

Available where books are sold.

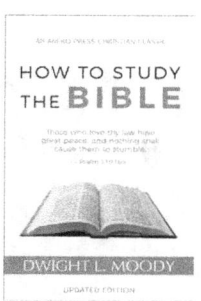

How to Study the Bible, by Dwight L. Moody

There is no situation in life for which you cannot find some word of consolation in Scripture. If you are in affliction, if you are in adversity and trial, there is a promise for you. In joy and sorrow, in health and in sickness, in poverty and in riches, in every condition of life, God has a promise stored up in His Word for you.

This classic book by Dwight L. Moody brings to light the necessity of studying the Scriptures, presents methods which help stimulate excitement for the Scriptures, and offers tools to help you comprehend the difficult passages in the Scriptures. To live a victorious Christian life, you must read and understand what God is saying to you. Moody is a master of using stories to illustrate what he is saying, and you will be both inspired and convicted to pursue truth from the pages of God's Word.

Available where books are sold.

The Overcoming Life, by Dwight L. Moody

Are you an overcomer? Or, are you plagued by little sins that easily beset you? Even worse, are you failing in your Christian walk, but refuse to admit and address it? No Christian can afford to dismiss the call to be an overcomer. The earthly cost is minor; the eternal reward is beyond measure.

Dwight L. Moody is a master at unearthing what ails us. He uses stories and humor to bring to light the essential principles of successful Christian living. Each aspect of overcoming is looked at from a practical and understandable angle. The solution Moody presents for our problems is not religion, rules, or other outward corrections. Instead, he takes us to the heart of the matter and prescribes biblical, God-given remedies for every Christian's life. Get ready to embrace genuine victory for today, and joy for eternity.

Available where books are sold.

A Life for Christ, by Dwight L. Moody

In the church today, we have everything buttoned up perfectly. The music is flawless, the sermon well-prepared and smoothly delivered, and the grounds meticulously kept. People come on time and go home on time. But a fundamental element is missing. The business of church has undermined the individual's need to truly live for Christ, so much so, that only a limited few are seeing their life impact the world.

Dwight L. Moody takes us deep into Scripture and paints a clear picture of what ought to be an individual's life for Christ. The call for each Christian is to become an active member in the body of Christ. The motive is love for the Lord and our neighbor. The result will be the salvation of men, women, and children everywhere.

Available where books are sold.

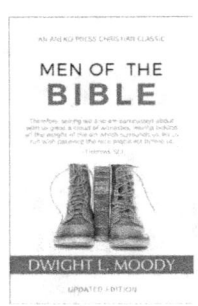

Men of the Bible, by Dwight L. Moody

When you wish to know something about godly living, where do you look? Is there a better place to look than to the men of the Bible? The Lord, in all His wisdom, left us with a wonderful textbook – the Holy Scriptures.

Some make the mistake of worshiping these heroes of the faith. Others make the mistake of only highlighting these men's weaknesses. Somewhere in the middle, though, is what God intended, and if our heart is right, we can learn all we need to know about healthy, rewarding Christian living from these incredible men of the Lord.

Available where books are sold.

The Ten Commandments, by Dwight L. Moody

The ten commandments are not popular today. Atheists want them nowhere in sight. Many Christians say they are outdated. But Dwight L. Moody challenges us to take a closer look. Which of the ten commandments can we honestly say are not good? Which of the ten commandments can we break and not suffer the consequences, both here and in eternity?

This book will challenge you to examine God's rules for life. God doesn't ask anything of us that is difficult or unreasonable, and this is certainly true with Jesus Christ as our strength and the Holy Spirit to guide us. This book is a challenging yet refreshing look at some of the oldest, most well-known words of God.

Available where books are sold.

Secret Power, by Dwight L. Moody

No other power on earth can quicken a dead soul except the same power that raised the body of Jesus Christ out of Joseph's sepulcher. And if we want that power to quicken our friends who are dead in sin, we must look to God and not to man to do it. If we only look to ministers, if we only look to Christ's disciples to do this work, we shall be disappointed. But if we look to the Spirit of God and expect that power to come from Him and Him alone, then we shall honor the Spirit, and the Spirit will do His work.

Available where books are sold.

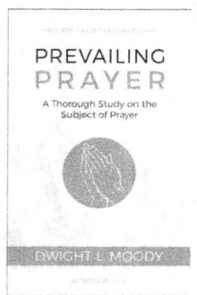

Prevailing Prayer, by Dwight L. Moody

This book is a comprehensive study on the subject of prayer, and will show you that there are nine elements which are essential to true prayer. These elements are as follows:

> Adoration, confession, restitution, thanksgiving, forgiveness, unity, faith, petition, and submission.

Dwight Moody expounds on these nine attributes in this volume, using illustrations and stories to validate what he is saying and to help make the truths in this book stick.

Available where books are sold.

Pilgrim's Progress, by John Bunyan

Often disguised as something that would help him, evil accompanies Christian on his journey to the Celestial City. As you walk with him, you'll begin to identify today's many religious pitfalls. These are presented by men such as Pliable, who turns back at the Slough of Despond; and Ignorance, who believes he's a true follower of Christ when he's really only trusting in himself. Each character represented in this allegory is intentionally and profoundly accurate in its depiction of what we see all around us, and unfortunately, what we too often see in ourselves. But while Christian is injured and nearly killed, he eventually prevails to the end. So can you.

Available where books are sold.

The Pursuit of God, by A.W. Tozer

To have found God and still to pursue Him is a paradox of love, scorned indeed by the too-easily satisfied religious person, but justified in happy experience by the children of the burning heart. Saint Bernard of Clairvaux stated this holy paradox in a musical four-line poem that will be instantly understood by every worshipping soul:

> *We taste Thee, O Thou Living Bread,*
> *And long to feast upon Thee still:*
> *We drink of Thee, the Fountainhead*
> *And thirst our souls from Thee to fill.*

Come near to the holy men and women of the past and you will soon feel the heat of their desire after God. Let A. W. Tozer's pursuit of God spur you also into a genuine hunger and thirst to truly know God.

Available where books are sold.

www.ingramcontent.com/pod-product-compliance
Lightning Source LLC
Chambersburg PA
CBHW070137080526
44586CB00015B/1733